# Foundations
## for the
## Christian
## Life

John G. Gill

PREPARING
THE WAY
Publishers

*"Making ready a*
*people for the Lord."*
Luke 1:17

2121 Barnes Avenue SE
Salem, OR 97306  USA

First Printing, April 2002

Published by

**PREPARING**
**THE WAY**
Publishers

**2121 Barnes Avenue SE**
**Salem, OR 97306 USA**

All Scripture quotations are from the
NIV unless otherwise indicated.

Cover design:  Clint Crittenden

ISBN 1-929451-11-3
Library of Congress Catalog Card Number 2002103838

Printed in the United States of America

# DEDICATION

To Dianne,

*. . . this is now bone of my bones,
and flesh of my flesh . . .*
(Genesis 2:23 NIV)


# INSPIRATION

In her presence, without knowledge or intent,
Kelly Marie Murdock
has made a difference in our lives.

# FOREWORD

John Gill is immensely practical. He cuts to the chase quickly and succinctly. If you're looking for long, complex, extended theological treatises, don't use this book. If you're looking for basic, down-to-earth understanding and enlightenment, this is perhaps the best foundations course you could use.

Getting the right start is important. Many of us started our Christian journey much like buttoning a shirt, but not getting the buttons and holes lined up correctly. The shirt still covers us and provides warmth, but it's not right. It doesn't fit right, and it doesn't look right. Over the years I have personally spent a lot of time unbuttoning and re-buttoning my doctrinal shirt. John's foundations book would have saved me lots of wasted time.

Several seekers at the Drug and Alcohol Re-hab Ranch where I serve as Chaplain have proven the effectiveness and practicality of this excellent resource. If you are a disciple maker, or desire to follow Jesus more closely, this book can be used of God as an excellent resource in your life.

Frank Smith

*Frank Smith is the spiritual director of the Green Oak Ranch at Vista, California. Green Oak is a vibrant rehabilitation center for drug and alcohol abusers. The work is an outstanding success. Rarely does a week go by that men and women are not brought to Jesus and, as is the custom, taken immediately to the swimming pool for baptism. Frank is also an apostle in the home church movement. He has outreaches in many places in the United States and Taiwan.*

# CONTENTS

# INTRODUCTION

In spite of the fact that bookstores are full of materials for new Christians to study, it has seemed to me that another approach is needed. Over a period of thirty years of intense involvement in the Church of Jesus Christ, it has become more and more clear to me that what we have been doing has not consistently produced either lively stones or a beautiful temple for the Lord. As of this moment in time, the Bride of Christ is not prepared for the wedding feast. Certainly there are many faithful and fruitful Christians in the body of Christ, but the fact remains that there seem to be many more who are neither faithful nor fruitful. The result is a nearly paralyzed church, incapable of presenting a unified, holy witness to the world.

I know very well that education is not the answer to spiritual problems. On the other hand it should be equally clear that if we do not know who we are in relation to God, we will experience severe difficulty in reaching fulfillment in that unknown role. And if we do not have a proper foundation, we cannot build well on it. It has seemed to me that it has been right at the beginning of our relationship with God that we have stumbled. It is my experience that salvation has often been preached incompletely and that our response has been either called out wrongly or not at all. Consequently, our church buildings are full of people who have incomplete and faulty foundations. Many believe that they are in Christ who may not be so, and many who are in Christ do not understand what is required of them once they are in Christ.

## Errors and Omissions

We have had a policy of *easy believism* in place in evangelical circles for many years. Evangelists and pastors have made it as easy as possible for people to enter the church. Altar calls often require only the furtive raising of a hand while *every eye is closed*. Sometimes they don't even call for that much public exposure. You can do it over the phone to a stranger or in your heart without any witnesses. The call itself is often totally non-threatening. You just *invite Jesus into your heart* or you *accept Him as your personal Savior*. Perhaps someone will someday give me Scripture references for those calls. Often repentance is omitted. With such a start, is it any wonder that many find no reason to behave any differently than they did before their *experience*. And, as a consequence, it is not surprising that we hear people, who are supposed to be Christian leaders, saying things like "I can't accept a God who allows children to suffer" or "God requires me to love you but not to like you" or "Of course abortion is bad, but we have to deal with the practical realities of life." Such talk comes from people who have a profound lack of understanding of God and no idea at all of who they are in relation to Him. Many have plugged into *pie in the sky by and by* without much in the way of present consequences or requirements. Without throwing away the pie, for it surely is there, can we not address the meat and potatoes of the present?

Although I am not addressing the performance of evangelists in this book, I do have some things to say about the content and presentation of the altar call. First, there must be a clear call for repentance. Repentance is required. Second, there must be a clear public commitment. Allegiance to Jesus must be proclaimed before men. Third, the call is for submission to the Lordship of Jesus, not for lining up to get a present of salvation. Salvation does result and it is a gift, but it is not given to heathens. It is given to the bond-servants of the Lord Jesus.

One of the most unfortunate results of the *sloppy agape* approach to evangelism and foundations is that people are led to expect all of the benefits of being a child of the Most High God without leaving the kingdom of the world and without fully entering the Kingdom of God. The entire thrust of Scripture is one of the victory experienced by God's people over whatever comes into their life by the power and authority of God through perseverance in faith and obedience. But, the lack of understanding and application of these principles has led to desires for instant gratification without cost. It is distressing beyond measure to listen to *faith* teachers who have the effrontery to order God to fulfill promises according to their understanding. The Scripture is filled with the promises and guarantees of God for His people. Nowhere is the image more compelling than in the parables concerning seeds, plants, growth, and fruit. The seeds of the Word of God are sown in fertile ground. They are cultivated, fertilized, and watered. The conditions for growth are met. In time, with care and perseverance, they produce fruit. We are eligible for every benefit of God when we become Christians. Some of them come soon while others take longer; all of them require submission and obedience to the King.

## Scriptural Basis

The sixth chapter of Hebrews, the first three verses, gives the only place in the Bible that specifies what the foundational teaching—in fact what the Christian initiation process—should be. I have therefore used that as the core of this teaching. I am indebted to Ted Walker, pastor of Church On The Rock, Little Rock, Arkansas, for allowing me to study the foundation course that his denomination uses, which is based on that same Scripture. I have adopted the style format, that is, lesson and then response, without appropriating the content or flow of the lessons.

In addition to the six elements covered in that passage of Hebrews I have added four more lessons and a Bible study suggestion. The first lesson, *What God?*, came from the study of recent pastoral problems with new Christians.[1] In past times, most Americans were rather familiar with what we mean when we talk about God. Unfortunately, the world and the devil have been busy evangelizing. Concepts of God that are foreign to Christianity can be found everywhere including inside the church. There are people who bill themselves as Christians who accept gods that are more like Buddhist, Islamic, or Hindu gods than the God of the Bible. For that reason I have devoted a chapter to the explanation of the nature and character of our great and almighty God. For new Christians who come out of a more or less conventional *nominally Christian* environment, this chapter may not be necessary, but it is better to have it than to proceed from false assumptions. If your new convert has in the back of his mind that our God is one of many gods, or that he can aspire to be just like God or a part of God by certain actions or prayers, it will be extremely difficult to make progress as a Christian.

The second lesson covers the identity of Jesus. If we are to submit to Him, we need to know who He is and what submission means. The next lesson deals with what the Scriptures are and why we can rely on them. At this point the lessons pick up Hebrews 6:1 and follow it for six sessions.

The final lesson in this study covers the part of Hebrews 6:1-3 which deals with the thoughts expressed by the following phrases, "... *and go on to maturity ... And God permitting, we will do so.*" I have titled it "In Him We Live and Move and Have Our Being." This lesson is on the church, the Christian community, and how to live and grow in it. It is my hope that the Scriptures and the suggestions made here will continue to help new Christians toward greater faith and more abundant fruit in their lives. Of course, the ultimate objective is to contribute to the fulfillment of the prophecy of Revelation 19:6-8:

> Then I heard what sounded like a great multitude, like the roar of rushing waters and like loud peals of thunder, shouting:  "Hallelujah!  For our Lord God Almighty reigns. Let us rejoice and be glad and give Him glory! For the wedding of the Lamb has come, and His bride has made herself ready.  Fine linen, bright and clean, was given her to wear." (Fine linen stands for the righteous acts of the saints.)

---

[1]*Where Do We Go From Here?* by Ralph W. Neighbors Jr., Touch Publications, Inc., Box 19888, Houstohn, TX 77224, 1990.

# WHAT GOD?

## Here, There, Everywhere

The recent history of popular culture has very nearly become a study of comparative religions. Hardly a day goes by but that some musician or actor doesn't give us a lecture on what he or she believes is the true religion. Ecologists and sociologists enter their opinions as well. Although politicians tend to keep clear of *dangerous* controversy as much as possible, they too will enter the field of discussion of religion as long as they can stay away from endorsing or being friendly toward Christianity. The rules of political correctness demand that all public figures be hostile toward Christianity. With all of this activity and discussion, the air is full of conflicting ideas. If we do not know something about the contending concepts, our minds will be full of confusion.

In no particular order, some of the varieties from which to choose include:

1) Atheism: The idea that there is no God of any kind. All is material, nothing spiritual. This is a foundational block of radical materialistic systems such as communism and socialism.

2) Polytheism: The idea that there are many gods with various interests and powers. Hinduism, Animism, Mormonism, Greek, Roman, and Norse mythologies as well as Oriental ancestor worship are brands of polytheism.

3) Pantheism: The idea that everything is God. Materialism and spiritualism blend. Individuality does not exist. Various brands of Buddhism, nature worship, *New Age* theosophy and meditational *self-realization* religions are generally pantheist.

4) Monotheism: The idea that there is one God. Judaism, Christianity, Islam, and Satanism are monotheistic (one God).

5) Self-Deification: The idea that the only importance is personal pleasure. Hedonism, Utilitarianism, and Dianetics are versions of this expression.

This is not the place to examine in detail all of the claims of the various philosophies. We will restrict ourselves to the major points of Christianity.

## The Complexity, Beauty, and Order of the Cosmos

Look around you. Everywhere you will see the evidence of intelligence and order in the material cosmos. The most insignificant weed on the side of the road is a marvel of functional, technical design that any engineer would be proud to call his own. From the greatest star systems through the world of plant and animal biology to microbiology and continuing to the tiniest universe of electronic particles, everything works together in predictable order. It is a great, complex, and brilliant God who has had the power and ability to create all of this. He wants us to know that and has displayed it before us with great splendor. The Bible says it in several places. Please read the following passages:

He alone stretches out the heavens and treads on the waves of the sea. He is the Maker of the Bear and Orion, the Pleiades and the constellations of the south. He performs wonders that cannot be fathomed, miracles that cannot be counted (Job 9:8-10).

Can you bind the beautiful Pleiades? Can you loose the cords of Orion? Can you bring forth the constellations in their seasons or lead out the Bear with its cubs? Do you know the laws of the heavens? Can you set up His dominion over the earth? (Job 38:31-33)

Do you not know? Have you not heard? Has it not been told you from the beginning? Have you not understood since the earth was founded? He sits enthroned above the circle of the earth, and its people are like grasshoppers. He stretches out the heavens like a canopy, and spreads them out like a tent to live in (Isaiah 40:21-22).

. . . since what may be known about God is plain to them, because God has made it plain to them. For since the creation of the world God's invisible qualities—his eternal power and divine nature—have been clearly seen, being understood from what has been made, so that men are without excuse (Romans 1:19-20).

The two passages from Job are very interesting historically. The book of Job is thought to be the very first one put down in writing. It comes from an earlier oral tradition when the village minstrel or poet was the tribe historian. This person was responsible to memorize all of the important historical facts of the tribe and sing them for the people at many occasions. The Pleiades, Orion, and the Bear are constellations of stars in the sky. So we can see that over two thousand years before Jesus was born (about 4000 years ago) the men of the Bible understood some very important astronomic facts and were able to relate these facts to God and His creative powers. You must understand that people at this time had no telescopes, and there was no such thing as astronomy except possibly in China and Egypt.

The passage from Isaiah reinforces the fact that the men of the Bible had an understanding of creation derived from observation of the world around them even without the advantage we have of great scientific technology. Finally, Paul the apostle sets it out for us. It seemed to him, as it does to me and surely does to God, God is obviously present and active in all that is around us. All it takes is a little thought and consideration. Can you not see Him?

## Personality

"Cogito ergo suum" is a very famous Latin quotation. It means, "I think, therefore I am." Another thing that it infers is that we can know some things because of other things that came first. When I see daylight I know that the sun is up because of my prior knowledge of the sun coming up. When it is night I know that it will be light after a while because of the same reason; I have seen the sun come up many times. I know a great many things from the experience of them; I do not need proof every time. In fact, the weight of experience then becomes a measure of empirical proof of the things that keep on happening in my life and the lives of the rest of the population of the world.

One of the facts of the cosmos is personality, especially in mankind. I do not have to prove to you that there is personality in mankind. It is there for you to see and experience every time you are with another person. A great theologian, Francis Schaeffer, called this the *mannishness* of man. Whether or not you can measure it or quantify it in any way does not take away from it. Man is different from all other entities. He can think and judge and remember in completely abstract ways. He can act perversely, against his own interests. He can act unselfishly, sacrificially in favor of another person, or a completely abstract cause. He can love and/or hate rationally or irrationally and sometimes simultaneously. No matter what the psychologists or evolutionists might say, man is just different from anything else there is and there is no natural, physical explanation for it.

But, of course, we have an explanation for it. The reason is found in Genesis. Read Genesis 1:26-27:

> Then God said, "Let us make man in our image, in our likeness, and let them rule over the fish of the sea and the birds of the air, over the livestock, over all the earth, and over all the creatures that move along the ground." So God created man in His own image, in the image of God he created him; male and female he created them.

Each time that God had finished with His daily task of creation, He looked it over and appraised it. On the first five days He said "it was good." On the sixth day, after He had created man, Genesis 1:31 says, *"God saw all that he had made, and it was very good."* God made everything there is, and it is good. God made man in His own image and likeness (with mannishness, personality) and that is very good! It is very important that we all remember that God didn't make any junk. His creation (you and me) is very good!

So, now we can extrapolate backward and forward and get some more ideas of what our God is like. He is personal. He dealt with our first parents individually and personally. As you read through the Bible you will see that God has dealt with everybody in history on a personal basis. More than that, as you interact with other Christians and as you interact with God yourself, you will discover that God deals with you on a personal basis as a loving father. The following Scriptures will reinforce the fact that God is a personal God who deals with you individually:

- Genesis 3:8-9
- 1 Samuel 3
- Jonah
- Acts 23:11
- Deuteronomy 11:1-7
- Job 42:1-6
- John 14:6-14
- Revelation 3:19-20

Our God is an omnipotent creator. He is personal and active. He is a loving father and totally trustworthy. But I don't have to prove any of those things. God is able to do that for you, and He will. I am proud to present to you the God of the universe: almighty, eternal Yahweh; who was, and is, and is to be!

## DIGGING DEEPER
### Here, There, Everywhere

1. Can you identify which religions promote the following beliefs:

You can become a god_____

When you die, you will become another being _____

When you die you become a god to your children ____

_____

Plenty of booze, drugs and sex is the way to go _____

_____

You and everything else are the result of time
plus random chance _____

God is omnipotent, creative, and personal _____

_____

*Note: You may not know all of these answers but you should learn them over time. As a Christian you should know what Christian doctrine is as well as what your enemies are doing to attempt to ruin you.*

2. What does political correctness say about Christianity?

_____

_____

## The Complexity, Beauty, and Order of the Cosmos

3. What is Orion? _____

4. How would Isaiah (prox. 700 B.C.) know that the earth is round? _____

_____

5. Have you observed the natural world and seen God?

_____

6. Please explain _____

_____

_____

_____

7. Do you have a theory as to how the universe came into being? _____

8. Please explain _____

_____

_____

_____

## Personality

9. Is there any difference in nature between you and a whale?

_____

10. Please explain _____

_____

_____

_____

11. Can you explain what *mannishness* means to you?

_____

_____

_____

12. Do you have any similarities to God? _____

13. Please explain _____

_____

_____

_____

_____

14. Do you think God can speak to men? _____

_____

_____

15. Can God speak to you? _____

_____

_____

16. Have you ever experienced God in a personal way?____

_____

17. Please explain _____

_____

_____

_____

LESSON TWO

# THE IDENTITY OF JESUS

## Opinion Polls, First Century Style

In a limited area, Jesus was a famous man in his own time. The limitations were natural ones. There was no television or radio to broadcast what was happening on a daily basis. There was no Sunday newspaper with an Opinion-Editorial section to discuss and analyze the public people and events of the times. Mr. Gallup was not around to ask Ebenezer and Obadiah what their opinions were about political and social issues. But Jesus was famous in Israel all the same. After he started his ministry as an itinerant preacher, he traveled all around the countryside on foot and talked to thousands of people both individually and in groups. Over a period of about three years he had talked to enough people and done enough things to make an impression on them. What do you suppose they thought about him?

Read the following verses in your Bible.

| Reference: | Person(s) |
| --- | --- |
| Matthew 16:13-17 | Apostle Peter |
| Luke 9:18-20 | Apostle Peter |
| Mark 12:35-37 | King David |

21

| | |
|---|---|
| James 1:1 | Apostle James |
| Romans 1:1-6 | Apostle Paul |
| Philippians 2:5-11 | Apostle Paul |
| John 20:24-29 | Apostle Thomas |
| Luke 3:15-18 | John the Baptist |
| John 1:29-31 | John the Baptist |
| Mark 1:23-24 | Demons |
| Luke 8:26-28 | Demons |
| Mark 5:1-10 | Demons |
| Luke 4:33-34 | Demons |
| Luke 4:41 | Demons |
| Matthew 28:12-13 | The Jewish Elders |
| Matthew 27:54 | The Roman Guards |
| Matthew 3:16-17 | God |
| Isaiah 42:1-4 | God |
| Luke 3:21-22 | God |

You should read each one of the verses above slowly and carefully and let them sink into your whole being. Perhaps you will want to memorize some of them. It is good to be able to remember that everyone who was acquainted with Jesus at the time of his work in Judea was in agreement. The Jewish elders who had Jesus put to death agreed with the apostles. Those elders were forced to make up a lie to account for the disappearance of Jesus' body. The demons, screaming with pain, had to agree with God. John the Baptist agreed with the Roman soldiers. This man Jesus was and is God. Isaiah foretold it hundreds of years before. King David prophesied it hundreds of years before. God became a man and came to live among us. He is Jesus.

## Jesus Identifies Himself

Jesus talked to many people about why He had come to be a man and do the things He did. Many of the things He said were written down and saved for us in the Bible. There are many people who have different opinions about what

Jesus was doing. Some say He was a great moral teacher but no more. Some say that He was a great prophet but no more. Others say that He was a great example of how to live but no more. It is interesting and curious to note that nobody ever accuses Jesus of being a criminal, a charlatan or a corrupt manipulator, even those who deny that He is the God-Man. Who do you suppose that Jesus claimed that He was?

Jesus referred to himself as the *Son of Man* on numerous occasions (Matthew 24:30, Mark 2:28, Luke 17:26, John 3:13-14). Although Jesus never made the connection directly, a passage from Daniel (7:13-14) describes the *Son of Man* as the coming King of the final Kingdom. He also responded to the term *Son of David*. This was a title that could only belong to the Jewish Messiah. When Peter named him as the *Christ* (anointed of God), the Son of the living God, Jesus did not object and even went on in a way that confirmed it in Matthew 16:15-20. On yet another occasion Jesus had a conversation with Thomas about His identity. Read John 14:1-14. In this passage Jesus declares Himself to be identical with the Father.

However, the clearest and most profound example of Jesus' declaration of who He was (and is) may be found in the book of John. Read John 8:12-30. In this passage Jesus refers to himself in a very unique way in verses 24 and 28. In verse 24 He says ". . . *believe that I am* . . ." and in verse 28 He says ". . . *know that I am* . . ." In both cases the translators have added words which you will probably find in brackets in your Bible. Those words do not belong there. Words in brackets or in italics in your Bible are always words added by translators to try to make things more understandable. Sometimes they don't make them more understandable. What Jesus said was, "*I am*" in both cases. This is the title God used when He identified Himself to Moses (Exodus 3:14). God said my name is "*I AM.*" Jesus said "*I AM.*"

Jesus used the same words to describe Himself in John 8:58. This time the translators have been faithful to the original. Jesus said, *"Before Abraham came to be, I AM!"* His meaning was clear to the Jewish officials. Since they were determined to find Him guilty of blasphemy, they picked up stones to throw at him. In John 13:19, the same sort of wording occurs. Jesus again says, *"I AM."*

Next read John 18: 5-8. At this time the soldiers and priests, led by Judas, were coming to arrest Jesus. Jesus identifies Himself twice. Here again the translators have thrown in an extra word *he*. Jesus said *"I AM"* twice. On the first occasion, the power in the declaration of the Name of God overcame the whole contingent, and they fell down before Him. Just think of what He could have done if He had desired? But from all of this the point should be clear. Jesus identified Himself as the Son of God, as identical with the Father, as God.

We should be equally clear about what we believe to be the true identity of Jesus. He gave us no alternatives such as *great teacher, prophet, or perfect example.* He declared Himself to be the Son of the Living God, the great I AM. It is clear that either Jesus was what He claimed to be or He wasn't. A man who claims to be God, unless He is God, cannot make any claim to goodness. He must be one of three things. He could be a madman on the order of one who claims to be a poached egg or a banana. He could be a great charlatan, out to gull the public for personal gain, power, or prominence. Or, He must be God. No other choice is available.

## The Work of Jesus

John the Baptist proclaimed, *"Repent, the kingdom of heaven is near"* (Matthew 3:2). Jesus came and proclaimed, *"The time has come. The kingdom of God is near. Repent and believe the good news"* (Mark 1:15). In the book of Luke the description of Jesus at His home town of Nazareth is recorded in 4:16-21. He recalled a passage from Isaiah 61:1-2, *"The good news of freedom, recovery, release; the year of the Lord's favor."*

The opening of Jesus' ministry in the book of John has a dual thrust. It is found in John, Chapter 2. The first thing Jesus did after His baptism was to make an abundance of very good wine for a wedding party at the request of His mother. The second thing He did was to go to Jerusalem and violently clear out all of the cheap hucksters in the temple.

All of these events have a common theme which is the proclamation of the Kingdom of God and the revelation of the King of that Kingdom. The time has come for the Kingdom of God to be established and the King has come in power and authority to do it!

Let us not divide up the presence of Jesus and highlight only His role as Savior. We say, "Have you accepted Jesus as your personal Savior?" That is far too narrow. It has been projected through history that God would establish a Kingdom which He would reign over personally. Now Jesus has come and says *Yes, the Kingdom is here and I am the King and you can be in it!* He says that the Kingdom is comprised of just such folks as you and me, and He will personally take care of all of our needs for deliverance, healing, freedom, and even wedding parties. Repent and come in. He is the Lord of every aspect of life. His primary work is to be our King.

Along with being King, Jesus is many other things. He is a busy King. Now read Isaiah 42:1-4. Then read Isaiah 61:1-3. Finally read Isaiah 53:1-12. In these passages you will see the work of Jesus. It is a personal work in each individual and it is a corporate work in His people. It is also a universal work in the world. His work is to save, restore, and regenerate by His own sacrifice, His own power and authority.

## Our Response to Jesus

Read Hebrews 9:14, 22 and Philippians 2:5-11. In these passages we see the salvation work of Jesus. But it isn't automatic. It doesn't overwhelm you without permission or knowledge. It requires repentance and submission to the

King. Acts 2:36-39 covers the call to repentance. Luke 6:46-49 and John 15:12-14 explain what Jesus means by submission to His Lordship. It is critical to living a productive and happy Christian life to make these things very clear right up front. Repent means change your mind and turn away from sinful, worldly, ungodly behavior and attitudes. It doesn't mean be sorry for it although that is part of it. It means turn away from it and stay away from it. Submission means acknowledgment that you are bought and paid for by the blood of Jesus. You are now a bond-slave of the King. Yes, He is your friend and your brother, too. But He is your King and master first, and you are bound to obey Him completely. Understand that there is no other course. Now read Luke 10:18-20 and Revelation 21:1-8. We will belong to the devil or we will belong to Jesus. We will obey one or the other. No matter which one we choose, we will end up accounting to Jesus. The alternatives are very plain. They are Jesus or death. My friend, we know that Jesus is the One to choose, don't we?

## DIGGING DEEPER
### Opinion Polls, First Century Style

1. What is the best description of the Kingdom of God?

_____

_____

2. What is our textbook for this study?

_____

3. Who did the apostle Peter say that Jesus was?

_____

4. Who did the apostle Thomas say that Jesus was?

_____

5. Compare what the Roman guard, the demons, and God the Father said about who Jesus was. Write any differences that you find.

_____

_____

_____

6. Why did the Jewish elders pay the guards a large sum of money?

_____

_____

_____

7. In the verses that you have read for this study, we have quoted the opinions of people who were His friends, some who were His enemies, and others who were just observers. What conclusion did they draw as to the identity of Jesus?

_____

_____

_____

_____

8. From the evidence that you have right now, who do you say that Jesus is?

_____

_____

## Jesus Identifies Himself

9. Who do you think the *Son of Man* is that is described in Daniel 7:13-14?

_____

_____

10. In Matthew 16:15-20 and John 14:1-14 can you conclude that Jesus agreed that He was the Son of the Living God and that He was one with the Father?

_____

_____

11. Would you say that Jesus was claiming to be God when He said that *"Anyone who has seen me has seen the Father"*?

_____

_____

12. How many times did Jesus apply the divine name *"I AM"* to Himself in the book of John?

_____

13. What kind of a person would it take to say he was God if he was not?

_____

_____

14. Fill in your opinion. I believe that Jesus is:

_____

_____

_____

## The Work of Jesus

15. What did Jesus declare as His message when He began to preach?

_____

_____

_____

16. What do you think is included in the Kingdom of God?

_____

_____

_____

17. Read John 18:33-37. Are you prepared to listen to this King Jesus?

_____

_____

18. How do you expect the work of King Jesus to affect your life?

_____

_____

## Our Response to Jesus

19. Explain what you understand about repentance.

_____

_____

20. Explain what you understand about submission to Jesus.

_____

_____

_____

_____

21. What are your options in how to live your life?

_____

_____

_____

22. Do you understand that salvation means coming into the Kingdom of God and that the only way that you can do that is by repentance from works leading to death and submission by faith to the King of that Kingdom which is Jesus?

_____

_____

_____

23. Have you repented and submitted to Jesus?

_____

24. If your answer to question 23 is _no_, would you like to do that right now?

_____

_If you are now ready to enter the Kingdom of God, please be sure to get together with your instructor or another Christian for prayer and be welcomed into the Kingdom._

25. If you have already repented and submitted to Jesus, please give a brief description of how that happened.

_____

_____

_____

_____

_____

_____

_____

## The Trinity

You have been introduced to Father God and His only Son Jesus. You may have heard that our God is a trinitarian God—that is, He is three yet one. It means that there are three persons or personalities in a single God. God is one yet also three. You will ask, no doubt, how that can be? It is a good question. It can be so because it *is* so. It cannot be understood fully or explained. It is said that a Roman Catholic order of scholarly brothers, the Dominicans, once took on the task of studying the Trinity so that they could explain it. After four hundred years of careful consideration they rendered their report. "The Trinity is a mystery," they said. There are many things in life that are mysterious and unexplainable. It is not because they are spooky or weird even though they might seem so. It is because we are presently incapable of full understanding. The Scripture says, *"No eye has seen, no ear has heard, nor has it even entered into the mind of any man what God has prepared for those who love Him"* (1 Corinthians 2:9). Why should it be unusual or weird that we would not be able to understand all that God is or is capable of doing? How arrogant we are to think that we should always be on an intellectual, not to mention spiritual, level with the Creator of the universe!

Although we will not dwell on the scriptural proofs of the existence and the deity of the Holy Spirit in these lessons, we will cover His ministry and activity in your life. The *plurality* of God is evident from the first chapter of Genesis where God say, in verse 26, *"Let **us** make man in **our** image, in **our** likeness . . ."* to the Revelation of John with its multiple references to the *Son of Man*, the *Faithful and True Rider*, the *Lamb*, the *Lord and His Christ*, the *Spirit*, the *Father* with the *Alpha and Omega* interchanging with them at various times. As you study the Bible, you will find more and more of the presence of the Holy Spirit. As you hunger more and more for the presence of God in your life, you will personally experience the work of the Holy Spirit along with the Father and Jesus. It is a process, a journey, a learning and growing experience.

There are many people in the world today who will try to talk you out of the existence and the deity of the Holy Spirit. Some will even try to convince you that Jesus is all alone, that there is no Trinity. For the most part those arguments come from people who have not experienced the undeniable power of the Holy Spirit in their lives. What they have not got for themselves, they would try to deny even exists. It is unfortunate but true. Do not get too excited about such things. God is prepared to show Himself true in all things, including the Holy Spirit, with all of the gifts and ministries that flow from Him. It is unnecessary to get in a big flap. Guard your heart, pray, study the Scriptures, and stay close to other Christians. God will take care of the rest. Trust Him.

# THE AUTHORITY
# AND RELIABILITY OF SCRIPTURE

## A Brief History

The Bible is actually a collection of many books. In fact, it can be called a complete spiritual library. It is "Everything you always wanted to know about God and the cosmos but didn't know who to ask." The books of the Bible began to be put into written form about 1500 years before Jesus was born although some of them were in existence before that time. Before men began to write on clay tablets, sheepskins, or parchment, they had what is called an oral tradition. Certain people in the tribes were charged with the responsibility of memorizing important facts and traditions and reciting them at various times. The book of Job and portions of Genesis were kept in that form until the time of writing began.

Moses is credited with the writing of the *Torah*, the first five books of the Bible. Then others wrote and collected the writings for the many centuries up to the First Century after Jesus' birth. The Bible used by most evangelical Christians contains thirty-nine books in the Old Testament and twenty-seven books in the New Testament. Roman Catholics, Orthodox, and other Christians recognize some additional writings as *canonical* as well. For the most part, the writings which you have in your hands right now are recognized by all Christians everywhere as true and without error.

There have been disputes through the ages over what writings are considered *canonical*. This is a term which means rule or standard. Although the disputes have been vigorous and lengthy, the result has been a consensus of Christians around the world that the Scriptures, that is the books of the Bible, are the certain word of God and may be believed without question. It is also agreed throughout most of Christianity that the Scriptures are inerrant but not exhaustive. That means that there is nothing false in them but that there is some additional truth that is not in them. It is important to be clear that although there is additional truth that is not in the Bible, there is not different truth in other places. It is further agreed across Christianity that all Christian truth must be in agreement with the Scriptures as they were written in their original languages. The judgment of the Church has been that the Bible was inspired and formed in men by the Holy Spirit just as it was written down and has been preserved throughout the years.

In our time, the preservation of the Bible may not seem to be such a remarkable thing. We have such wonderful ways of printing, copying, photographing, recording on magnetic or laser media, and otherwise preserving documents, that it doesn't surprise us to find a book kept as our Bible has been. However, times have changed a lot.

Consider that there are, in addition to Roman Catholic and Orthodox sects, some 26,000 different professing Christian bodies or denominations. Every one of these units represents (shamefully, I am afraid) a difference between brethren that is strong enough to cause separation. Yet almost without exception, all of them agree on the inspiration and inerrancy of the Bible. All of that disagreement and yet agreement on this point. That is miraculous!

Although we now have means of printing, copying, and preserving the written word with almost absolute accuracy and reliability, it was not always so. Until the Fifteenth Century, every writing was just that, a writing, a hand-writing with quill and parchment or even more primitive methods and media. If you wanted a copy of a book or the Bible, someone had to sit down and copy it by hand. This was a very laborious and time consuming enterprise, and it was thoroughly boring as well. Clerks in monasteries drowsed through this task for centuries. Even after the advent of movable type, invented by Gutenberg, every printed word was hand-set, letter by letter, until the middle of this century. It is a miracle that the Bible could survive intact and unchanged, but it did.

Consider also the enemies of the Gospel. Those who have not come into the light of Christ are the enemies of Christ as you and I once were. Some of these are dead set against the Gospel and go to great lengths to falsify or discredit it. But even after thousands of years and hundreds of thousands of attacks, no attack has prevailed. The Bible has been compared to every sort of historical account and always has been found to be accurate and true. Some of the enemies of the Bible delight in finding new sources of ancient historical writings such as the Dead Sea Scrolls in hope that they will discredit the biblical accounts, but they never do. The biblical accounts always hold up.

Finally, consider the testimony of the saints. Millions of faithful Christians have gone through the world and before them the faithful Jews. In many times it would cost you your very life to believe in the Scriptures. Yet time after time the *people of the Book* have stood firm in the face of persecution and death. Why do you suppose that this is? It is due to the ministry of the Holy Spirit in the lives of believers. The same Holy Spirit who was responsible for inspiring the biblical authors also gives assurance to the hearts of believers so that they may stand firm in the face of attack.

In the end it is the Holy Spirit who insures the inerrancy of the Bible. It is perfectly reasonable to assume that the God who made the world and all that is in it; He who made man in His image and allowed man to learn God's ways and write them down; that same God who enabled men to invent writing and printing presses; He is able to preserve His word through the ages. He is able to preserve His word through time, languages, translations, and vernacular expressions. Remember that. He is able.

## What does it Say?

Your Bible is divided into two main sections, the Old Testament and the New Testament. The Old Testament covers the world and God's relationship with it and with His people prior to the birth of Jesus. The New Testament covers the birth, life, death, and resurrection of Jesus as well as the testimonies, teachings and activities of the apostles during the First Century. The origin of our faith is in the Old Testament and the Jews up to the time of Jesus' taking the Kingdom from them. From that time on, God's dealing with His people and with the world is vested in the New Testament and the Church He founded on Jesus Christ. The authority of God's word has been conferred upon the Christian Church under the kingship of Jesus.

Open your Bible to the book of 2 Timothy, Chapter 3, verse 16. In this book, the apostle Paul was writing to his disciple Timothy, whom he had taught and trained, in order to encourage him. See what he has to say about the Scriptures.

The New Testament had not yet been written when Jesus was involved in His ministry. Jesus called the Scriptures *the law*. Read Luke 16:17 for Jesus opinion of *the law*. Now look at Matthew 5:17-18. Here again Jesus comments on *the law*. Of course the accounts that were written about Jesus' life, death, and resurrection became accepted as Scripture later.

Read the following verses carefully:

| Psalm 119:9-11 | Hebrews 4:12 |
| 1 Thessalonians 2:13 | Matthew 4:4 |
| John 15:3 | Ephesians 5:25-26 |
| Isaiah 55:11 | John 15:7 |

Determine from the verses above what you can expect to get out of reading the Bible.

Now go back to the Old Testament and read Deuteronomy 6:4-9. In this passage Moses was recounting and explaining *the law* to the Israelites. He was telling them what God thought about his *word* to them. Note carefully the importance that God places on His Word.

Go on to the Psalms. Read Psalm 33:4, 119:105, and 138:2. The Psalms are songs sung by the Israelites during their celebrations. See what God told them about His word and how to revere it. Further on in Proverbs 30:5, note how Solomon commented on God's Word.

Finally we come to the books of the prophets. The prophets were men who were called by God to be his spokesmen to the Israelites and to the world. The word *prophet* means *one who speaks for another*. It doesn't mean *future forecaster*, although that was what God told them sometimes. God was mainly concerned about correcting their behavior through the words of the prophets. The principles behind these words apply to us today as much as they applied to ancient Israel. Over time you will read all of the books of the prophets many times, but to begin, read and carefully consider the book of the prophet Jonah. Think about the word of the Lord to Jonah and how it applies to you.

There are hundreds of Bible verses that tell us the Scriptures are God's words to us. Those listed above are just a few of them. You will want to read these and the others in a consistently planned way every day in order to get what God wants you to get from them.

## The Logical Results

You have now read enough of God's Word to know that God expects you to respond to His word with obedience. He has covered every aspect of human life in the pages of the Bible. It is, without question, the guide to the most successful life possible. It will take you some time to sort out the difference, but the success is measured in far different ways than in the world and is far more satisfying than that of the world.

The Bible covers far more than religious practices. It addresses family, friendships, work, money, sex, and leisure activities as well as doctrinal beliefs. As I said at the beginning of this lesson, the Bible covers everything you always wanted to know about God and the cosmos but didn't know who to ask. Now you know Who to ask.

## Suggestions for Bible Reading

Unless you have some idea of what you are going to do when you pick up your Bible, you may just meander around aimlessly and reduce its effectiveness. You should have some sort of plan even if it is not very elaborate. There are many plans for Bible reading and study. Here are some suggestions that may help you.

First, be diligent about it. This is one of the few areas of Christian life that should be approached diligently. What that means is that you should have a regular schedule of dealing with the Scriptures and stick to it. Discipline yourself to the time of day and amount of time that you spend as well as the type of approach that you take.

There are at least three ways that you will benefit from reading the Bible:

1. You should study the Bible from the point of view of learning doctrine. With a good study guide, a concordance, or Bible dictionary you can look up various

subjects and see what God has been saying over the centuries to His people about it. You should examine all of the Scriptures on any given subject before you decide to formulate a doctrine. There is a tension in the Scripture that will confuse you if you do not take all of it into account. Then remember to read Eccles. 3:1-8. You will see in this passage that God has a timing for all that He says and does. What is appropriate at one time is not at another time. Keeping this in mind will help you when you are judging what God is telling you to do. This kind of study should be done approximately once a week and should be done with the help of a mature and fruitful Christian tutor.

2. Background study. You should study the Bible as a historical document. You can see the history of the world from God's viewpoint. You can see the history of God's dealing with all of mankind and with his specially chosen people. You can see what kind of people that have inhabited the planet and have been chosen by God to be His people. This kind of study should be done on a weekly basis with little or no guidance. A good Bible dictionary will give you clues as to where to find things to study.

3. Repetitive immersion. The Bible has some unusual characteristics. One of those characteristics is that you can never exhaust everything that it has for you. Every time that you re-read passages of Scripture, new things will come to you. One reason for that phenomenon is the maturing process that you will go through. At this point in time you can understand a certain amount. A year from now, as you are faithful, you will discover that you have increased in your understanding. This process never seems to stop. In order to be immersed in God's Word time after time, you need a program that will take you through every word in the Bible over and over again. I consider this the most important way to read your Bible.

You could just start from the beginning and go through to the end and then repeat the process. Some people do that and are happy with it. Here is another suggestion. There are sixty-six[1] books in the Bible that I use. These books contain 1224 chapters. These chapters may be divided into four units as follows:

- Old Testament from Genesis through Job—514 chapters

- Psalms, Proverbs, Ecclesiastes, Song of Songs—211 chapters[2]

- Prophets—249 chapters

- New Testament—260 chapters

Starting with the first book in each division, read one chapter from each division each day. Thus you will read four chapters from diverse parts of the Bible each and every day. If you follow this pattern you will read the Old Testament through in about a year and a half. The Psalms, etc., will be read about one and three quarter times each year. The Prophets will be read one and one-half times per year, and the New Testament will also be read about one and a half times per year. Using this pattern, do not look for anything special, just let the Word speak to you and then spend a few minutes after each passage in contemplation of it.

Understand that it is very important that you do this or something like it, and if you do, it will improve your life dramatically. Now read the introductory verses at the beginning of the last book of the Bible, Revelation 1:1-3:

> The revelation of Jesus Christ, which God gave Him to show his servants what must soon take place. He made it known by sending His angel to His servant John, who testifies to everything he saw—that is, the Word of God and the testimony of Jesus Christ. Blessed is the one who reads the words of this prophecy, and blessed are those who hear it and take to heart what is written in it, because the time is near.

We can assume that much needed blessings for us are associated with the reading of all of the Scriptures. How much nearer is the time today than when John wrote that sentence? Happy Scripture immersion!

## DIGGING DEEPER
### A Brief History

1. Describe what the Bible is.

_____

_____

_____

2. How old is the oldest part of the Bible?

_____

3. What does *canonical* mean?

_____

_____

4. What do you think *inerrant* means?

_____

_____

5. Did more than one man write the Bible?

_____

6. How were all writings done before the Fifteenth Century?

_____

_____

_____

7. Approximately how many different Christian bodies are there?

_____

_____

8. What do documents like the *Dead Sea Scrolls* show about the Bible?

_____

_____

_____

9. What is the final guarantee of the accuracy and reliability of the Bible?

_____

_____

_____

_____

## What Does it Say?

10. What are the two divisions of the Bible?

_____

11. What times and events does the Old Testament cover?

_____

_____

12. What times and events does the New Testament cover?

_____

_____

13. What are four ways in which the Scriptures are useful?

_____

_____

_____

_____

14. Did Jesus teach about the Scriptures?

_____

15. Did Jesus say that the Scriptures would be almost completely fulfilled?

_____

16. Write the things that you can expect from study of the Bible according to each of the following verses.

Psalm 119:9-11 _____

Hebrews 4:12 _____

1 Thessalonians 2:13 _____

Matthew 4:4 _____

John 15:3 _____

Ephesians 5:25-26_____

Isaiah 55:11 _____

John 15:7 _____

17. Does God consider His Word to be important? (read Psalm 138:2) _____

18. What does the word *prophet* mean?

_____

_____

19. What did God tell Jonah to do?

   _____

   _____

20. What did Jonah do?

   _____

   _____

21. Explain the lessons that you have learned about God's character and His expectations from reading the book of Jonah.

   _____

   _____

   _____

   _____

   _____

22. Do you have a systematic plan for reading the Bible?

   _____

23. Please explain your plan.

   _____

   _____

   _____

   _____

   _____

## The Logical Results

24. Do you believe that the Bible contains *the words of life?*

_____

_____

_____

25. Do you have any difficulty in believing any parts of the Bible?

_____

_____

_____

26. Make a list of the major concerns in your life. One by one you will want to look up what the Bible has to say about these things. After reviewing this lesson with the one helping you, you may go on to Lesson Four.

_____

_____

_____

_____

_____

_____

_____

_____

## An Important Note

Now that you have completed the preparatory lessons on God, the Identify of Jesus, and the Validity of Scripture, you are prepared to move on to this next phase. This may be called the Christian-initiation phase. Every part of it is important or the Holy Spirit would not have included it in Scripture. One of the great problems in the Church today is that of incomplete, carnal, or stagnant Christians. We have all seen those who have been content to attend church services fairly regularly for years but who show little or no fruit in their lives. Some of these even engage in seriously sinful behavior. Somehow, they have never been plunged into the life of God in a way that would radically change them forever.

The following lessons have been prepared for you with that in mind. We do not want to take responsibility for any teaching which does not penetrate or with lives that do not change. We believe that you are entitled, as a new child of the Most High God, to the most complete, most powerful tools that are available. We think that there are no classes of Christians like upper class, middle class, and lower class. All true Christians are radically upper class, and here is where we begin. The inclusion and the order of the following six lessons have been determined by the best authority in the world—God. Hebrews 6:1-3 describes what the author (the Holy Spirit) considers to be the proper items and the proper order for the basic things of Christian life:

> Therefore let us leave the elementary teachings about Christ and go on to maturity, not laying again the foundation of repentance from acts that lead to death, and faith in God, instruction about baptisms, the laying on of hands, the resurrection of the dead and eternal judgment. And God permitting, we will do so.

The term *baptize* is practically only used in a religious sense in these days. However, in Jesus' time it was a word used in commerce as well. It was used in the cloth-dying business and in the making of swords and other armor. When a piece of cloth was plunged into the vat of hot dye, it came out changed. When a sword was heated and hammered and then plunged into the quenching water, it came out radically hardened; changed. Just such a radical kind of life change was the expectation for every person plunged (baptized) into the life of Christ. That is our expectation also. Come, plunge in!

---

[1]In the Roman Catholic Bible there are seven additional books which we term the *apocryphal books* in the Old Testament. There is a diversity of opinion as to their canonicity which we will not discuss here. If you are reading a Roman Catholic Bible it will take you a few additional days to cover the Old Testament.

[2]Actually, there are only 201 chapters in this unit. However, Psalm 119 is very long, and I divide it into parts of two stanzas each. It takes eleven days to read it all. I recommend this since young Christians might be bored with the law theme in the beginning and tend to go through it too quickly, but more mature Christians will appreciate it and want to spend a bit more time with it.

# REPENTANCE FROM WORKS
# LEADING TO DEATH

## What is it?

Read the following passages carefully:

| | |
|---|---|
| Matthew 3:1-2 | Matthew 4:17 |
| Mark 1:14-15 | Acts 2:37-38 |
| Mark 6:12 | Luke 13:3, 5 |
| Acts 3:19 | Acts 17:30 |

Can you see that God puts a premium on repentance? Most of us have heard the word *repent* for all of our lives. Over a long period of time, because of familiarity and lack of care, the word has been eroded and its meaning distorted for many people. In the Greek language, repent means to turn around or to change your mind about your actions and therefore your behavior. This is an action word. It involves doing something. It does not include the moral and mental processes that lead up to it.

## How do We do it?

The two things leading up to repentance are the understanding and admission of guilt and godly sorrow. These always come before repentance. We have assumed, because of our sloppy use of words, that to repent meant *to be sorry.* Now, you can be sorry for a multitude of reasons. You might be sorry because you are embarrassed over being discovered doing something shameful. You might also be sorry because you are fearful over getting caught and being punished for some act. It is also possible that you would be sorry because you had done some damage or injured someone. All of that would be good, but none of it would be repentance and God wants repentance.

Sorrow enters into the scene after the understanding and admission of guilt. So, it is important for us to know that we are guilty of offenses against both God and man. It might not be clear to you what God considers sin. So turn to Galatians 5:19-21 and get some examples. We are equipped with a conscience from the start, but sometimes it becomes *seared* by repetitive, evil behavior. That is, sometimes we become so used to doing ugly things that we don't consider them to be evil any more. But, if we will be honest before God, He can and will cut through even the most seared conscience which will bring us a sense of our own guilt. Once we have understood and admitted our guilt we are able to experience godly sorrow.

Godly sorrow is the emotion and attitude that we assume once we have understood that every sin, every evil deed, is not only an offense against other people, it is an offense against God. God, totally pure and sinless, has created us to be in loving fellowship with one another and with Him. Everything we do against one another, we do against God. In addition to that, every denial of God's existence, benevolence, and power is an insult to Him. That also is sin, and we all have been guilty of it. As the Scripture says, *"All have sinned and come short of the glory of God"* (Romans 3:23). Understand that even the smallest sin, the slightest offense, disqualifies us from fellowship with God.

So then, it must be clear to us from the beginning that we are and have been guilty of sin. We have offended one another and a holy and sinless God. In our natural state we are unfit for friendship with God, and this must cause us great, godly sorrow. That sorrow, then, will certainly lead us to repentance. Our whole heart and soul will be torn by sorrow, and we will then *turn away* (repent) from our sinful behavior.

## *Good* but Deadly Works

But repentance must include even more than that. It is not only sinful behavior that requires repentance. Included in *works that lead to death* are acts that attempt to replace the grace of God with the works of men. In our time, there are sects and cults who will tell you that you can do things that will make you holy and perfect apart from God. These things might include some forms of prayer, self denial, generosity, or kindness. Apart from Jesus Christ, none of these things will have any effect. Jesus said clearly in John 14:6, *"No one can come to the Father except by me."* Understand that you cannot get into friendship with the Father except in the company and with the permission of Jesus. So, every self improvement apart from God is an offense to God. It is us saying, "It's okay, Jesus, but I can handle it myself. I don't need you." But the Scripture says, *"All of us have become like one who is unclean, and all our righteous acts are like filthy rags"* (Isaiah 64:6). We must repent from even the so-called *good* things that we have been doing to make ourselves look good and perfect ourselves without God.

Do you feel as though you are being stripped down to nothing? That's good. That is the way to start this process—clean. If you have not done it yet, sit down and inventory your life. Mentally, or even on paper, list as many as you can remember of the things that you have done to hurt people and offend God. Also list all the things that you have done in the *do-gooder* category that had nothing to do with Jesus. Even gather up the times that you wanted to do rotten or selfish or self-promoting things but didn't because you didn't get the opportunity or didn't have the nerve. The

Scripture says that even your ugly thoughts offend God. See Matthew 5:28. Be diligent about this and merciless with yourself. Hopefully, you will only do this once, so it is worth doing well.

Now read Proverbs 28:13. See here the contrast between one who will repent and one who will not. Go back to Isaiah 6:1-5. In this passage Isaiah has been chosen to be a prophet of God. See how he realizes what kind of a man he is compared to a holy God. You are invited to make the same comparison. When you were invited to come to Jesus, you may have been somewhat aware of your sinfulness. Hopefully by now you are aware of your utter sinfulness and complete incapacity to be God's friend on your own. This is no small thing. It is the first in a set of building blocks and without it, the rest of the building cannot be built.

## The Rest of the Story

You will note that there has been no mention of Adam & Eve, the snake, or the apple. "What about original sin," you might ask? Good question. Here is where you get a big, big bonus at no extra cost. You see, it was this *original sin* that disqualified every man, woman, and child on the face of the earth from friendship with God. Eve was disobedient to her husband and didn't believe him when he told her what God had decreed. Adam was the real culprit, however. He had the word straight from God but he buckled in front of his wife and the snake, rebelled against God's command, and ate the fruit. Read Genesis 2:15 to 3:19 to get this story straight. This combination of rebellion acted like a genetic defect in all of mankind. We were all disqualified from birth from God's Kingdom.

Even so, there is nothing that you or I can do about Adam and Eve. We didn't do the sin so we can't repent from it. So what is the point of all this? It is merely to point out to you that you are, or were, completely helpless in your sinful state. You couldn't do anything about it if you wanted to and you probably were even incapable of wanting to. You were the member of a degenerate race (all mankind) with no way out. Any sacrifice you might offer to God would be contaminated by your resident sinful nature.

And that is where Jesus comes in. When you repent you also add in your helplessness and turn to the only One who can help you—Jesus. When you do that you find that Jesus has taken Adam's sin and your sin with Him on the cross. He has seen your helplessness and your sin and has taken all of the punishment that you deserve. Read John 18 and 19 for starters. He got your beating. They pulled out His beard and punched His face instead of yours. It was His head that they crammed the crown of thorns onto, and it was His knees that got scraped to the bone on the pavement, not yours. They slammed the nails through His hands and feet, and when He died they poked His side with the spear. It was His blood that was sloshed around all over the city of Jerusalem. It should have been yours, but it wasn't. It was His. And that is how you and I get in to the Kingdom. We slide in by means of simple repentance and His blood. If that isn't a good deal, there are no good deals.

## The Price for the Blood

You are that price. Jesus was willing to do all of that for you. He did it literally to purchase you from the devil. See Acts 20:28. Buying your freedom from the devil is an interesting thing. You see, the devil had no use for you nor could he do anything with you. He just wants to destroy you (1 Peter 5:8). When he got the rights to you it was strictly for the purpose of taking one long, last swim in the Lake of Fire with you. See Revelation 20:10 and 21:8. We will address all of the goodness of the life in the Kingdom of God at a later time. For now, remember this. Let it be burned into your brain. When you come to Jesus because your guilt has caused you godly sorrow—and your godly sorrow has resulted in God allowing you repentance—you are bought and paid for totally by Jesus and you now belong to Him. You are now a bond-servant of the Lord. You owe Him your life. You owe Him everything. It is not symbolic; it is real. You have chosen life over death, and you belong to the giver of life for twenty-four hours of every day for the rest of your life.

## DIGGING DEEPER
### What is it?

1. What is a condition that *you must meet* in order to come to Jesus for salvation?

_____

_____

2. Refer to at least one Scripture verse that supports your answer to question one.

_____

3. Define the word *repent*.

_____

_____

_____

### How do We do it?

4. What are two things that come before repentance?

_____

_____

5. Are you guilty of sin?

_____

6. Whom does sin offend?

_____

7. Who has not sinned?

_____

8. Is a natural person fit for friendship with God?

_____

## *Good* but Deadly Works

9. What kinds of things can you do to earn salvation?

_____

_____

10. Describe the only path leading to the Father.

_____

_____

11. To what can we compare all of our righteous acts that are done without Jesus?

_____

12. What can you bring from your life before Jesus that will help you enter the Kingdom of God?

_____

## The Rest of the Story

13. Who committed the original sin?

_____

14. What was it?

_____

_____

_____

15. What was the effect of that sin?

_____

_____

16. What can you do about it?

_____

17. Who can help you with your problem?

_____

18. Who else can help you with that?

_____

19. Have you done what is necessary for Him to help you?

_____

## The Price for the Blood

20. What is the result of the deal that gets you free from sin?

_____

_____

21. What is your status in the Kingdom of God?

_____

_____

22. What do you have that is yours alone?

_____

23. What belongs to Jesus?

_____

_____

The old man in all of us wants to retain ownership and control of everything, of something, of anything. Repentance includes the divesting of your self of *everything* in Jesus' favor. You must start out with and retain the attitude that you are totally sold out to Jesus. It is the only attitude that will provide you with real freedom. Galatians 2:20-21 says:

> I have been crucified with Christ and I no longer live, but Christ lives in me. The life I live in the body, I live by faith in the Son of God, who loved me and gave himself for me.

It is by faith that you have come to repentance, though you probably didn't know it. In your next lesson you will learn more about this faith that you have received and exercised toward Jesus.

# FAITH IN GOD

## What is Faith?

Here are a few scriptural synonyms for faith, taken from *Strong's Exhaustive Concordance*: (Old Testament Hebrew) Firmness, trustworthiness, established, security, fidelity, stability. (New Testament Greek) persuasion, credence of religious truth, assurance, belief, fidelity. Now look at the definition of faith that the Scripture gives in Hebrews 11:1,

> Now faith is being sure of what we hope for and certain of what we do not see.

Go to the book of Hebrews, and read all of Chapter 11. You could look up all of the people who are referenced in this chapter. They are all characters from the Old Testament. Their stories are told in detail in their parts of the Bible. You should make a resolve to look them all up some time soon, so as to build up your own faith. It is always encouraging to read or hear about someone who acts heroically.

All of the people mentioned here have two things in common. First, they believed that they had heard from God in some way. Whether they had got it from a voice, a vision, or from some other person, they were convinced that what they had heard was from God. Second, they believed what they had heard strongly enough so that they modified their behavior. In some of the cases, believing and acting was expensive. It cost some of these heroes of the faith everything, sometimes even their lives.

So, if we are to express what we mean by faith in our own words, what are we to say?

- It is belief that we can know what God says.
- It is belief that He is reliable and dependable.
- It is belief that what God says is important.
- It is belief that He means what He says.
- It is belief that God does what He says.
- It is belief that what God says overrides every other thing.
- It is belief that no price is too high to pay for being in agreement with God.
- It is belief that adhering to what God says will come out right in the end no matter how things look to us.

## What is *Not Faith*?

The premier example of *not faith* or unbelief in God is found right at the beginning of mankind, in Genesis, Chapters 2 and 3. Read from 2:15 through 3:13. One thing that you might miss is the fact that God didn't tell Eve to stay away from the tree of the knowledge of good and evil. He told that to Adam before Eve was made. So it must be that Adam told his wife what God had said to him. Now, when the serpent came to them (you see in verse six that he was there, too), she was a second-hand witness; but Adam, who had the word straight from God, was silent. I have often thought in the past that the first sin was Eve's since she took the fruit. But she wasn't as responsible as Adam, and Adam didn't even open his mouth (except to take a bite). Eve was guilty of disbelieving her husband and of manipulative behavior. Adam was guilty of rebellion against the direct and clear instructions of God. Even more than that, he was guilty of abandoning his wife in the face of evil. He let her take a bite first, perhaps to see if it was safe. He was a coward and a rebel. His behavior was exactly the opposite of what we discussed earlier.

- She questioned whether or not God had truly said what He said.
- She questioned whether God had told them the truth.
- She questioned whether her husband had told her the truth.
- He did not believe what God had told him.
- He thought that something was more important than what God had told him.
- He would not correct his wife in her error.
- He allowed his wife to take charge of the situation in ignorance.
- He allowed the serpent and his wife to bring him into rebellion.

Together, they made us incapable of friendship with God. They were the sum total of the human race in existence at that time, and they went into rebellion together making them and all of their offspring (which includes us) outsiders to the Kingdom of God.

You can read some other scriptural accounts of unbelief. The Old Testament is full of examples. The Jews were chosen by God to be His people and to be the instrument of bringing all people to God, but they failed again and again. They sinned often in many ways because they did not believe what God told them. Their biggest and most offensive sin was idolatry. Read 1 Kings 11:1-13 and 12:26-30. These are only two of the examples of rebellion by the Jews against God, but they are very serious ones. Solomon's unbelief resulted in the breakup of his kingdom. Jeroboam's unbelief ultimately resulted in the destruction of Israel and the elimination of ten of the Jewish tribes from history.

Now turn to Matthew 21:33-44. In this situation, Jesus was speaking to the chief priests and elders of the Jews. These were the biggest and most important men in the land. They exercised both religious and secular power. They were representative of the leadership of centuries of the kingdom of the Israelites. They had failed to obey God many times. They had repented many times, and God had restored them. This time they went over the edge. They refused to believe in the Son of God—Jesus. They refused to accept the divine plan for complete restoration of man to friendship with the Father. They rejected God one time too many. God declared them out as a nation. From this time on they could enter the Kingdom of God in the same way that every other human being could do it. They could enter one at a time by the way of Jesus. (Read Romans 11, and you will see that the Jews will be brought back just like that, one at a time.) That is the result of *not faith*. That is unbelief and what it does.

## What About Me?

We have covered some really big examples of faith and lack of it. But, what about us ordinary people who don't control the destiny of the world? What about you and me? The reality is that you and I operate under the same rules as the others, the really important people. God considers you and me to be just as important as Adam or King David or Moses or Abraham. In fact, we have a distinct advantage over those Old Testament people. They didn't have Jesus yet, but we do have Him.

Here is the situation and the rules.

1) Romans 3:23 – *"For all have sinned and fall short of the glory of God."* We start out without friendship with God because of Adam, and it deepens because of our own sinful behavior.

2) Romans 3:20 – *"Therefore, no one will be declared right-eous in His sight by observing the law; rather, through the law we become conscious of sin."* We are unable to make amends with God for what has happened by being good or obeying commandments.

3) Romans 3:23-24 – *"For all have sinned and fall short of the glory of God, and are justified freely by His grace through the redemption that came by Christ Jesus. God presented him as a sacrifice of atonement, through faith in His blood."* Jesus Christ, having taken our punishment, has atoned to the Father for Adam's sins and ours by the shedding of His own blood. We can do only one thing—have faith that it works.

There is the cornerstone. We can believe that God said that Jesus could save us by shedding His blood for us. We can believe God when He says that there is no other way to become His friend, His child. We can believe that Jesus did shed His blood for us. We can believe that this process works for us. We can accept it as a done deal. We can't do anything. We can only have faith. Faith is our only asset. We can use it to gain salvation, allow it to grow for a full life, and depend on it for others. In the end, faith is all we have, and it is a gift of God. See Ephesians 2:8-10.

In relation to God, we must have the attitude portrayed by the Hebrew word *anawim*. The *anawim* are those who are the poor in spirit, those who are utterly dependent upon God for everything they have and everything they are, and who know it! —*Fr. Raymond Elam, OSA*

# DIGGING DEEPER
## What is Faith?

1. Write at least three words that are synonymous with faith from the biblical view.

_____

_____

2. According to Hebrews 11:1, is our hope sure?

_____

_____

3. Can we see the object of faith?

_____

4. In Hebrews 11:4, what is necessary in order to please God?

_____

5. What did Noah do by faith?

_____

_____

_____

6. What did Moses' parents do by faith?

_____

_____

_____

7. In Hebrews 10:39, what is the result of believing?

_____

_____

8. Did good things happen to all of the people mentioned in Hebrews 11? (Read verses 35-37 very carefully and thoughtfully.)

 

9. Do you believe that God has called you to Himself?

 

10. Do you believe that God *wants* to save you from sin and death?

 

11. Do you believe that God *can* save you from sin and death?

 

12. Do you believe that God *will* save you from sin and death?

 

13. Are you saved?_____

Is this faith? _____

## What is *Not Faith?*

14. Did Eve have direct knowledge of what God had said about eating the fruit?

 

15. Did Eve rebel against God?

16. What did Adam do when the devil said that God had lied?

_____

_____

_____

17. What did Adam do when his wife was in danger of death?

_____

_____

_____

18. When Adam saw that Eve did not immediately drop dead, what did he do?

_____

_____

_____

19. When God questioned Adam about eating the fruit, what did he do?

_____

_____

_____

20. Is it your opinion that you would consider Adam a reliable, trustworthy friend to have in a time of danger or trouble?

_____

_____

_____

21. Did Adam have faith?

_____

22. What was the result of Solomon's unbelief?

_____

_____

_____

23. What did Jesus do as a result of the unbelief of the chief priests and elders of the Jewish nation?

_____

_____

_____

24. Can the Jews re-enter God's Kingdom as a nation?

_____

_____

_____

25. Can Jews be saved today? _____

_____

_____

## What About Me?

26. Does God consider anyone better or more important than another? (Read Acts 10:34 and Galatians 3:26-29.)

_____

_____

27. Having read Romans 3:20-24 answer the following questions:

What percentage of mankind has failed to make it with God? _____

How many people can get right with God by working really hard at lots of good stuff? _____

What is the key to getting right with God? _____

_____

_____

28. What is your single asset before God? _____

_____

_____

Even the *faith* for salvation is a gift from God. See Ephesians 2:8-10 again.

# BAPTISMS:

# FIRST STEP–WATER BAPTISM

## Dispelling Confusion

Maybe you have heard some confusing teaching about the need or lack of need for baptism in water for Christians. Maybe you have also heard some confusing talk about how and when baptism ought to be done. Let us address these issues directly, with Scripture as our sole authority.

There is a story that goes like this: If you were way out in the Sahara Desert and became a Christian with nobody else around and no water within 100 miles, what would you do about water baptism?[a] In the same story, after a few days, what if another Christian came along with a canteen of water. What would you then do about baptism?[b] Now revise the story a little more. Say that you have with you a nephew who is brain damaged from birth. He is seventeen years old chronologically but mentally about four years old. He suddenly expresses a love for Jesus because he heard you praying and talking about Jesus. Do you baptize him,[c] and how do you do it?[d] What if you had in your growing party, a baby of six months that you knew was doomed to die with you of exposure and dehydration. Would you baptize her?[e] What would you do about baptism if you were in that same situation but you were bitten by a deadly snake and nobody could rescue you?ᶠ Would you baptize the others or be baptized in each of those situations and how would it affect your salvation? That is the real question—how does baptism affect salvation? Do we really need to be baptized or is it an option?ᵍ

The issue here is really one of obedience more than anything else. We will examine the Scriptures to see whether that is true or not. Read Matthew 3:1-17. Carefully note verses 11 and 15. In this passage we see several things. John the Baptist was calling the Jews to repentance and baptizing them for it. Jesus agreed so strongly with this that He came to John for baptism Himself. He ratified water baptism to *fulfill all righteousness* by submitting to it Himself even though He had no sin from which to repent. That same story is told in Mark 1:1-11 and Luke 3:1-22.

Now go to Matthew 28:16-20. In this passage, Jesus has been crucified and resurrected and is giving His final teaching to the apostles before He goes bodily to sit at the right hand of the Father. In this short saying are four very important items:

1) Verse 18, Jesus claims the authority he needs, that is: *"All authority in heaven and on earth has been given to me."*

2) Verse 19, Jesus directs (commands) the disciples to *"go and make disciples of all nations."*

3) Verse 19, Jesus directs (commands) the disciples to baptize the new disciples *"in* (or into) *the name of the Father, and of the Son, and of the Holy Spirit."*

4) Verse 20, Jesus directs (commands) the disciples to *"teach them to obey everything I have commanded you."*

If we truly believe Jesus and accept His authority, this passage is quite clear. New believers are to be baptized in water.

We can find further evidence in Mark 16:16. In this verse we see that Jesus demands that we believe and be baptized. Those who refuse will be condemned. Is that not clear?

But, let us now go further yet. Turn to Acts 2:36-41. This is the recounting of Peter's message on the Day of Pentecost. At the end of the preaching, his audience was deeply moved by what they heard. They knew that they needed to do something about it right away. What did Peter tell them to do? *"Repent* (turn your behavior around) *and be baptized in the name of Jesus Christ for the forgiveness of your sins."* Next look at Acts 8, in which two different stories are told about new believers' baptisms and Chapter 9 which records the conversion and baptism of the apostle Paul. More stories of new believers being baptized may be found in Acts 10, 16 and 18.

It should be quite clear by now that John the Baptist, Jesus, Peter, and Paul were all in agreement about baptism. It is an essential ingredient of the Christian life. We do it because Jesus said to do it. As bought-and-paid-for bond-servants, we need no other reason.

## The Right Rite at the Right Time with the Right Intent

We should note that there is no specified right way to baptize shown in the Bible. The inference is that most people were immersed in water, perhaps a river, a pond or something like that, but it is not stated. The word *baptize* in the Greek means "to make whelmed, fully wet; or to moisten." It has been traditional in some circles to immerse the new believer completely. In other places water is poured or sprinkled over the person being baptized. Terrific battles have been fought over which is the way. It cannot be ascertained from Scripture. If God found the issue of immersion or sprinkling to be a critical one in the life of a believer, could He not make it clear to us which He preferred? We should look at what it is we are doing and not so much the mode of doing it. Is it not the intent of the heart that God will see?[1]

The age of the person baptized and that person's ability to consent have also been points of contention in the Church for centuries. In every story showing baptism in the Bible, it is preceded by a faith decision and repentance. On the one hand it would seem that only those who are adults or those with sufficient adult reasoning power can make such decisions. On the other hand, in the cases of the lady Lydia and the Philippian jailer found in Acts 16, you will see that one person seems to have made the decision for each of the families. It looks as though Lydia decided and all those in her household were baptized. It would appear that when the Philippian jailer was converted, he led his whole house into baptism. Household or house (*oikos*) means a dwelling and those in it—more or less extensive and more or less related—including the possibility of men, women, children of all ages, servants and slaves, not withstanding mental or physical capacities.

So, what is the age and mental condition required for baptism? We can make educated guesses and well-reasoned inferences, but we cannot pin it down with certainty. It can become a highly subjective exercise, entangled in psychological considerations of maturity and judgment. Such debates will take us away from the issues of faith that are primary. Here again we ask ourselves about the intent of the heart which God examines. Let us keep that in mind when the subject comes up.

Ultimately, it is you and I who are addressed to make a decision. We can quarrel forever about ages, mental capacities, and the rites used for others. Important as they may seem, those are not the questions for most of us. For the most part, those arguments merely distract us from the real issue. The real issue for us is will we be obedient to the Lord and see to it that we are baptized? Will we assist others to be obedient to the Lord and teach them to obey what He has taught?

One man may believe sincerely that he has faith for his very young or even mentally disadvantaged children until they can have faith for themselves, and he is willing to guard them and teach them while they acquire that faith. Another may believe sincerely that he must wait until they can understand and accept the teaching themselves, and he is willing to guard them and teach them until that time. The most important item is that men and women shall have authority over and care for their children and lead them in righteous ways, carefully observing the duties and responsibilities of parents. Have faith that God can and will be just, righteous, and merciful. We need to *"guard our hearts as they are the wellspring of life"* (Proverbs 4:23).

## Gospel Tension

Let us now return to the little story that is at the beginning of this lesson. Please note that there are seven superscripted letters in that story. Please spend some time in prayer about each of those possibilities. Of course they are far-fetched. Of course they are very improbable. It is good for you to notice that. It is from far-fetched, improbable, worst case scenarios that much of the strife in the church originates. A fact is that almost all of us are able to be baptized by any method that we choose. Another fact is that God is not playing mind games with us. He is merciful and He is just. He is not looking for a way to slap you into hell when you aren't paying attention to the tricky details. If you ever come to a situation anything like that described in the first part of this lesson, you do your best to be obedient to God if it means baptism in saliva. As to the results, trust God. He is trustworthy.

## DIGGING DEEPER
### Dispelling Confusion

1. The following lettered spaces correspond to the super-scripted letters in the little story in the lesson. Please write any comments you have about each situation.

a _____

_____

b _____

_____

c _____

_____

d _____

_____

e _____

_____

f _____

_____

g _____

_____

2. Was it necessary for Jesus to be baptized?

_____

3. Does Jesus have the authority to tell you and me what to do?

_____

_____

4. In Matthew 28:20, what did Jesus say to do?

_____

_____

_____

5. In Mark 16:16, there is a reference to what happens if we refuse to be baptized.  What is it?

_____

_____

6. What do you find different in the way that John the Baptist, Jesus, Peter, and Paul dealt with baptism?

_____

_____

_____

_____

7. What is your status regarding baptism in water?

_____

_____

_____

## The Right Rite at the Right Time with the Right Intent

8. What is the best way to be baptized?

_____

_____

9. Who does baptisms?

_____

10. Having read Acts 16, assume that there was a slave in the Philippian jailer's household who had an infant son. Do you think that they baptized the baby?

_____

_____

_____

11. The Philippian jailer was a man, and Lydia was a woman. Did that make any difference in their decisions for their households?

_____

_____

_____

12. What would be a good reason to give for not getting baptized?

_____

_____

_____

_____

## Gospel Tension

13. Do you have anything to add to your comments in question one?

_____

_____

_____

_____

14. Read Acts 2:38-39 again. What will result if one is baptized?

_____

_____

_____

15. Read Romans 6:3-5. What will result from baptism for us?

_____

_____

_____

16. Read Galatians 3:26-29. You are baptized into what?

_____

_____

17. If you are obedient to do what you have been commanded by Jesus as well as you are able, is He trustworthy and able to save you?

_____

_____

_____

_____

---

[1]Some years ago I had occasion to serve a sentence in the San Diego County Jail. During that time I taught a nightly Bible study in one of the other inmate's cells. After a period of time, six inmates wanted to be baptized. We had no river, pond, or pool in the cell block. I instructed each of the inmates to get a large cup of water and, as we leaned out over the commode, I pronounced the words of baptism while we all poured out our cups. This was a full immersion sprinkling. Do you think those six men were truly baptized?

# BAPTISMS:

# CONTINUATION OF THE PROCESS

## The Holy Spirit

There is a word *heresy* which comes from the Greek word *hairesis*. In our time it has come to mean *one who believes wrongly about God*. We say that someone is a heretic if he or she believes something about God which is false. The original meaning of the word also includes in the meaning *anyone who picks and chooses wrongly what to believe*. In other words, you can be a heretic even when everything you believe is true, if you have not believed all there is to believe. If you leave important things out or somehow rationalize and explain them away, you are just as much a heretic as one who accepts things that are completely false. We live in a time that is full of heresy and heretics. There is a famous missionary named K.P. Yohannon who is busy establishing Christianity in the Far East. He is very successful at it, and he has commented on why Americans are not very good at it.

He says,

> In reality, I have come to see that many evangelical Christians don't really believe the Word of God. Instead, they selectively accept only the portions that allow them to continue living in their current lifestyles.[1]

These words will be increasingly important to you as you go along. You will be constantly bombarded by unbelief, disbelief, acceptance of error, and rejection of truth. In this lesson we will cover subjects that have become very controversial. It is so because there are some who say that believing in them is heresy or even from the devil. You must sort the arguments out for yourself in the light of God's Word and with the guidance of the Holy Spirit. The first topic to cause trouble is the baptism in the Holy Spirit.

Read Matthew 3:11, Mark 1:7-8, Luke 3:16, and Acts 1:5. Each of these passages of Scripture says that Jesus will baptize the believers with the Holy Spirit. In fact, it is Jesus Himself who states that they will be baptized with the Holy Spirit in the passage from Acts. It should be clear from this that there is such a thing as *baptism in the Holy Spirit.* The term is quite conventional and scriptural.

Now read Acts 2:38-39. Note that the Holy Spirit is to be a gift to all who repent and are baptized in water. Note especially verse 39 which says, *"The promise is for you and your children and for all who are far off—for all whom the Lord our God will call."* See how inclusive this language is—*"all who are far off—for all whom the Lord our God will call."* All, not some; *"ALL."* That is especially noteworthy, and so we want to emphasize it especially. All means all, not some, not most; it means all.

Go back to Acts 2:2-4. In this passage we see that the first disciples received the promise of the baptism in the Holy Spirit just as John the Baptist prophesied and just as Jesus promised. Now go to Acts 4:31. Here we see that, after the apostles and disciples prayed, the building was shaken, and they were all filled with the Holy Spirit again. By this we can see that the promise has been fulfilled to baptize believers in the Holy Spirit, and that it can happen more than once to the same people. There is one baptism, but there can be many fillings.

Now you should read the following passages: Acts 8:14-17, 10:44-48, and 19:1-7. In these verses you will read of the times in which Jews and Gentiles alike received the baptism in the Holy Spirit in several different situations. One time the people received the baptism in the Holy Spirit before they were baptized in water, which shocked Peter. This is a passage that ought to be read often. It shows that God does things to those He chooses, and He does them in His own way. Sometimes we are shocked when God violates our schedules and our systems. We should not be dismayed, but we are. Remember that God knows the end from the beginning. Everything He does is good and good for you. Relax when things go in a direction you do not understand. Relax and let God be God.

## Why?

When Jesus went back to the Father, He promised that He would send the Holy Spirit. In the Book of John from 15:26 to 16:15, Jesus told us some of what the Spirit does. Some other passages in the four Gospel accounts concerning the Holy Spirit are: Matthew 1:18-20, 12:31-32; Mark 3:29, 12:36, 13:11; Luke 1:15, 34-37, 67, 3:22, 4:1-2; and John 14:15-18, 25-26. You will profit from reading each one of these stories. Even before Jesus sent Him to be with us constantly, the Holy Spirit was active in the world and in the lives of God's people. He filled and empowered John the Baptist. He was responsible for the pregnancy of Mary and for her protection. He empowered Jesus to heal. He is the expression and action of God in the world today. To blaspheme Him is to cut yourself off from the life of God. Why do you suppose that God would continue to be so personal and intimate with mankind?

In the lives of believers and the teachings of the apostles, many other passages describe the Holy Spirit and what He does. Just a few of these will illustrate His ministry. Read Romans 5:5 and Galatians 5:22-23. Here we see that over time the Holy Spirit puts many good things into us. We call these things the fruit of the Spirit. Concentrate on remembering these things. The fruit of the Spirit will cure you of the ragged, jaded frazzle of the world around you.

Next look at 1 Corinthians 6:19. When we become Christians and receive the Holy Spirit, our very bodies become temples—holy places. The Holy Spirit lives right inside of us which makes us into very special creatures. In 1 Corinthians 2:10-16 we can see that, from inside us, where He lives, the Holy Spirit teaches us and reveals to us the wonders of God, and He also imparts to us the mind of Christ.

Further on in 1 Corinthians 12, the first 11 verses list some of the gifts of the Holy Spirit. Please read that. These are some, but not all, of the gifts possible to receive from the Holy Spirit. These are some that God has thought you ought to know something extra about, so He put them into this Scripture. List them on a piece of paper and think about them. These are abilities that God wants to have among His people so that they can be built up in His Kingdom. Notice very carefully that verse seven says, *"Now to each one the manifestation is given for the common good."* This is not the place to go into great detail about all of the gifts of the Holy Spirit. It should suffice to say that God has great and wonderful gifts for us to be used in great and wonderful ways. We will do well to want to be a part of everything that God does. It is all good and good for us.

Can you begin to see that God's plan always was to be intimate with men and women. He has desired to have men and women as special friends, beloved and intimate. But we are too fickle, weak-willed, and selfish on our own to be intimate friends of God. In the Old Testament there are several times when men were deathly afraid of God's presence because they were convinced that no man could come close to God and survive the experience. It is because of sin that this fear is present. Sin in the presence of God will be burned to a crisp (see Revelation 20:10-15 for a description of the Lake of Fire).

Since God still wants intimate friendship with us, He has provided the ways to get it. We already know that Jesus took our just punishment for all sin, and that fact gets us into the entry level condition to be in the presence of God. But we still need more. Read Romans 7, and you will see the picture of a man who wants to do right in the sight of God but cannot. What are we to do? Can we sin, repent; sin, repent; sin, repent forever? Are we to ride a spiritual roller coaster until Jesus comes? What do we do about the command of Jesus in Matthew 5:48 which is *"Be perfect, therefore, as your heavenly father is perfect?"* Has the Lord given us something to do which is impossible for us?

Of course He has not! We can see quite clearly that, although we ourselves are quite incapable of holiness on our own, the empowerment of the Holy Spirit makes all things possible. Jesus said so to His disciples. In Luke 18:25-27 Jesus compared the business of getting a rich man into the Kingdom of God with trying to stuff a camel through the eye of a needle. It is the same sort of job for you and me to reach perfection on our own merits. We can't do it, but God can and it isn't by magic either. It is a process that begins with our repentance. After receiving the free gift of salvation by faith because of the sacrifice of Jesus, we move on to baptism in water for the forgiveness of sin and to baptism in the Holy Spirit for the empowerment of the Christian to live the life of God.

In Acts 1:4-8, the Lord Jesus told the disciples,

> . . . do not leave Jerusalem, but wait for the gift my Father promised, which you have heard me speak about. For John baptized with water, but in a few days you will be baptized with the Holy Spirit . . . but you will receive power when the Holy Spirit comes on you; and you will be my witnesses in Jerusalem, and in all Judea and Samaria, and to the ends of the earth.

On Pentecost it happened to them. In Acts 2:1-12, we can read about the experience that they had. You and I are entitled to the same experience with the same results.

So, what's the problem? Millions of Christians around the world have shared this experience of God's grace. Many other millions have either refused or been steered away from this experience. The baptism in the Holy Spirit has become a point of division in the Body of Christ. The most common rationalization that you will hear is that, "God doesn't do that any more. That was just for the first Christians to jump start the church. We don't need it any more so God doesn't do it."

That statement should be rejected on two grounds. First of all, God never has stopped giving His Spirit to believers since that Pentecost. Throughout the ages there have always been Christians who have claimed the baptism in the Holy Spirit and exhibited the gifts and the fruits of the Spirit just as the Scripture says. Secondly, the Scripture, which is God's word to us, says that He will baptize us in His Holy Spirit. It says that once the Holy Spirit is given to us He will be with us forever. Read John 14:16. The Holy Spirit is actively with us now and has been since that Pentecost. It is absolutely certain that you will not be able to live a Christian life with any success without the fulness of the Holy Spirit. If you should choose to refuse the gift of the baptism of the Holy Spirit, you will be only partially initiated, seriously handicapped, and at least somewhat miserable for your whole life. Why in heavens name would anyone want that?

## How?

The reception of the baptism in the Holy Spirit is really quite simple.

1) Desire it.

2) Ask Jesus for it.

3) Wait for it.

4) When it comes, accept it.

It is no more complicated than that. Although some people may wish to lay hands on you and pray for you to receive the baptism in the Holy Spirit, that is not essential. It is certainly helpful to have other Christians around you to teach you things and answer your questions, but you may receive the Holy Spirit in power at any time and at any place, alone or with somebody. Some will also be quite insistent that you speak in tongues when you are baptized in the Spirit. Here is one of those gray areas. There does not seem to be an absolutely certain answer to the question, "Do all Spirit-baptized Christians speak in tongues?" Do not be intimidated or downcast if you do not speak in tongues immediately upon the reception of the Holy Spirit. On the other hand, do not fear or despise the gift of tongues or any other gift of God. It just happens that the gift of tongues seems to generate a lot of controversy. You are not praying for the gift of tongues but the gift of the Holy Spirit. The gifts and fruits of the Spirit will follow in due course. Remember 1 Corinthians 12:11 says, *"All these are the work of one and the same Spirit, and He gives them to each one, just as He determines."*

You will know when the Holy Spirit is working in your life; it will not be a secret to you. As 1 Corinthians 12:7 says, *"Now to each one the manifestation of the Spirit is given for the common good."* You will notice the manifestation and so will others around you. As you continue your study of the life of Jesus, you will recognize Him in your life. His character and His power will be more and more reflected in you. His character is described by the fruit of the Spirit, and His power is exampled in the gifts of the Spirit. You may think that such things are far above you or even arrogant to desire. Not so! It is what God wants for you. It is why He bought and paid for you in the first place.

## A Plurality of Baptisms

It is important to note that our basic Scripture, Hebrews 6:2, says "... *instructions about baptisms* ..." The word is plural indicating two or more baptisms but not establishing the exact number. We have already covered two of the baptisms—water and Holy Spirit. We should now note that there are even more baptisms than these two.

John the Baptist predicted that Jesus would baptize with the Holy Spirit and with fire in Matthew 3:11 and in Luke 3:16.

In Matthew 20:20-23 a discourse is described between Jesus and James, John, and their mother. Jesus tells them that He has an additional baptism to undergo (remember that He was already baptized in water and the Holy Spirit), and that they would also share in it. He did not name this baptism, but it seems clear that it was connected with His imminent suffering.[2] The same event is described in Mark 10:35-40, clearly noting an additional baptism to be undergone by Jesus and these Apostles. Still one more time Jesus refers to an additional baptism in Luke 12:50 without giving it a name. The context is clearly one indicating difficulty and suffering.

It would be foolish to attempt to develop a whole theology of additional baptisms from the references we have. It would be even more foolish to deny that they exist. We are prepared to be immersed in whatever it is that God has for us at any time. We know that what God has in store for us is good, even if fire and suffering are included.

# DIGGING DEEPER
## The Holy Spirit

1. Write down two places in the Bible where the baptism in the Holy Spirit is mentioned.

   _____

   _____

2. On what Jewish holiday was it that the first group of Christians were baptized in the Holy Spirit?

   _____

3. Who is speaking in the passage from Acts 1:5?

   _____

4. After the initial baptism in the Spirit can there be additional fillings?

   _____

   _____

   _____

5. Who may *not* receive the baptism in the Holy Spirit?

   _____

   _____

   _____

6. Is it possible to be baptized in the Holy Spirit before you are baptized in water?

   _____

   _____

   _____

7. Is it more important to be a Jew or a Gentile when you want to receive the baptism in the Holy Spirit?

_____

_____

8. Who does the baptizing in the Holy Spirit?

_____

9. If you heard a radio program with a very famous preacher telling people that the baptism in the Holy Spirit is from the devil or outdated or not necessary, how would you respond?

_____

_____

_____

## Why?

10. Has the Holy Spirit ever acted in your life?

_____

11. Can you briefly describe what happened?

_____

_____

_____

12. Write down some of the things that the Holy Spirit does from the passage in John 15:26-16:15.

_____

_____

_____

13. Write down the gifts of the Holy Spirit which you find in 1 Corinthians 12:1-11.

_____

_____

_____

_____

_____

14. Write down the fruit of the Holy Spirit which you find in Galatians 5:22-23.

_____

_____

_____

_____

_____

15. Write down which ones of the gifts and fruits of the Holy Spirit that you would rather _not_ receive.

_____

_____

_____

16. Please explain your answer to question 15.

_____

_____

_____

_____

_____

17. What is the purpose of the gifts of the Spirit according to 1 Corinthians 12:7?

_____

_____

_____

_____

18. What do you think that Jesus meant when He told us to become perfect (Matthew 5:48)?

_____

_____

_____

_____

19. Do you think that you can become perfect without the power of the Holy Spirit?

_____

_____

_____

## How?

20. If you have already received the baptism in the Holy Spirit, please describe your experience.

_____

_____

_____

_____

21. If you have not received the baptism in the Holy Spirit, please explain how you will go about receiving it.

_____

_____

_____

_____

_____

_____

22. Which of the gifts of the Spirit are specified in the Scriptures as essential to every believer?

_____

_____

_____

_____

23. Who decides which gifts you get?

_____

_____

24. If Jesus wants you to be like Him, how will you express His power in your life?

_____

_____

_____

_____

_____

_____

25. How will you show the character of Jesus in your life?

_____

_____

_____

_____

_____

_____

26. What is the source of your answers to questions 24 and 25?

_____

_____

_____

_____

[1]*Revolution in World Mission* by K.P. Yohannan, Creation House, 190 N. Westmonte Drive, Altamonte Springs, FL 32714, 1992.

[2]The NIV does not specifically mention baptism in this passage although it is clearly *baptism* in the original Greek. See Matthew 20:22-23, King James Version.

# LESSON EIGHT

# LAYING ON OF HANDS

## Healing and Deliverance

Evil entered into our world with the first man and woman. Sin and death, both physical and spiritual, have plagued mankind ever since. When Jesus came to live among us He demonstrated the power of God to liberate us from sin and disease. Time after time Jesus healed people from their diseases and liberated them from evil spirits. He did these things by ordering them done and by touching the afflicted with His hands. The description in Matthew 4:23-24 is typical of the ministry of Jesus:

> Jesus went throughout Galilee, teaching in their Synagogues, preaching the good news of the kingdom, and healing every disease and sickness among the people. News about Him spread all over Syria, and people brought to Him all who were ill with various diseases, those suffering severe pain, the demon possessed, those having seizures, and the paralyzed, and He healed them.

As He declared the gospel of the Kingdom of God, Jesus made it plain that He was expecting those who followed Him to do the same things that He did. Jesus ran a great *OJT* (On the Job Training) type of ministry. He did things in the way they ought to be done so that we could learn to do them by imitation. Read Matthew 10:1-8 and Luke 9:1-6. In these passages Jesus empowered His disciples to go out and do as He had been doing. Jesus was glad when they succeeded and disappointed when they failed. Read Luke 10:1-9, 17-21, and Mark 9:14-27. Now read John 14:9-14, and you will see what Jesus had to say about His followers doing the same as He had been doing.

It should be clear from these passages that Jesus expected the healing of sicknesses and deliverance from evil spirits to be a part of the Christian life. The power that Jesus intended to give to His followers comes through the gift of the Holy Spirit in the baptism of the Holy Spirit that we studied in Lesson Seven. One method of prayer for healing and deliverance is by the *laying on of hands*. In Mark 16:18, the Scripture quotes Jesus saying, *"they will place their hands on sick people, and they will get well."* The ones that Jesus was talking about was us, the ones who believe. Jesus laid His hands on many for prayer, healing, and deliverance and expects us to follow His example. Read Matthew 19:13-15; Mark 5:40-42, 6:5; and Luke 13:12-13.

## Commissioning for Service

The use of the hands is always significant. From earliest recorded history the extension of the open right hand has signified lack of hostility. The open hand, empty of weapons, is clasped as a sign of friendship. Open arms are a sign of joyful reception. Hugs, pats, and caresses are a natural and pleasant part of life. God goes even further. He has used the laying on of open hands for healing and deliverance, as we have seen, and also for the commissioning of His people for service, for the impartation of His spiritual power, and to designate their functions in His body, the church.

In Genesis 14, Abraham raised his hand to swear an oath to the King of Sodom, and in Chapter 24 Abraham's servant put his hand under his master's thigh in order to swear an oath to him. In Genesis 48 and 49 you can read how Jacob blessed and prophesied over his children, laying his hand on their heads. In Exodus 14, Moses stretched out his hands over the Red Sea, and the Lord parted the waters for him. Even the humblest Israelite observed the custom. In Leviticus 1:4 we see that the Israelite was to lay his hand on his sacrificial lamb before the Lord so that it would be acceptable as a sin offering.

In the book of Nehemiah we see how God transfers His power to us and says it is because *"His hand is on us,"* (see Nehemiah 2:8). In Ezekiel 1:3 and 3:14 the prophet declares that the hand of God was upon him as he began his prophetic ministry. Many, many instances of the placing of hands on men for good and for evil are found in the Old Testament. As Jesus exercised His ministry, He began to transfer power from the Levitical priesthood to the people; from God to men.

In Matthew 19:13-15 there is an interesting little story. There is no mention of what purpose there was in laying hands on the children, if any. We can put ourselves in the place of the children. Jesus just wishes to caress and bless us by the laying on of His hands. He blesses and empowers us with His Spirit as He lays His hands on us. After His death and resurrection, the Holy Spirit continued the blessing through the laying on of hands by the apostles and then by all believers.

The first impartation of ministry was by the laying on of the hands and prayers of the apostles described in Acts 6:1-7. This was the appointment of deacons for the church at Jerusalem. In Acts 8:14-17 we see the impartation of the Holy Spirit by the laying on of hands by Peter and John. In Acts 9:17 Paul has his sight restored and is filled with the Holy Spirit through the laying on of hands of a disciple named Ananias. In 1 Timothy 4:14 we read about the impartation of a gift to Timothy by the laying on of hands by the elders.

Although we are admonished in 1 Timothy 5:22 not to be too quick to lay hands on anyone, this is a practice that has come to us from the very beginning and is important to us today.

## Application

Some things to remember about laying on of hands:

1. Jesus appointed all of us to go and imitate Him. Paul said, *"Imitate me as I imitate Christ."*

2. Any Christian is eligible to lay on hands and pray.

3. If you want to lay hands on someone and pray for mission, ministry, ordination, or special giftings you should probably question whether or not God has given you the authority and specific direction to do that. If He has, go ahead. After all, God is in charge of all of these things, and He will grant only those things that are in agreement with His will.

Do not think that anyone else can do what you are called to do in the Body of Christ. Each one of us has certain duties, privileges, and responsibilities. The Body of Christ comes to unity and full stature as we exercise those functions.

## DIGGING DEEPER
### Healing and Deliverance

1. Is there any limitation on how God can do the things that He wants to do?

_____

_____

_____

_____

2. Does God want us to be free from sin and disease?

_____

*If you are having difficulty with these two questions, read Luke 4:14-21 and discuss it with your leader.*

3. Did Jesus heal a large number of people?

_____

4. Did Jesus also relieve people from oppression of demons or unclean spirits?

_____

_____

5. According to John 14:9-14, who will do what He has done?

_____

_____

_____

6. According to Mark 16:18, how will believers deal with sick people?

_____

_____

_____

7. Are you prepared to lay hands on people that you know and love and pray for them to be healed and delivered?

_____

_____

_____

## Commissioning for Service

8. Isaiah 2:4 says that there will be a time when men will *"beat their swords into ploughshares and their spears into pruning hooks."* Is there a connection to the use of our hands that you can see? Please explain.

_____

_____

_____

_____

_____

9. The open, extended hand symbolizes which:

   Peace _____

   Anger _____

10. List several kinds of situations in which men and women of God may lay their hands on people for different reasons.

_____

_____

_____

_____

11. Is power transferred to or applied to the person having hands layed on or is the exercise symbolic?

_____

_____

_____

12. What does it mean in 1 Timothy 5:22 when it says, "*Do not be hasty in the laying on of hands, and do not share in the sins of others. Keep yourself pure*"?

_____

_____

_____

_____

## Application

13. Explain what it means to *imitate* Jesus in laying on of hands or in anything else.

_____

_____

_____

_____

_____

*"Sacrifice and offering you did not desire, but my ears you have pierced; burnt offerings and sin offerings you did not require. Then I said, 'Here I am, I have come—it is written about me in the scroll. I desire to do your will, O my God; your law is within my heart' "* (Psalm 40:6-8).

# THE RESURRECTION OF THE DEAD AND ETERNAL JUDGMENT

## Resurrection of the Dead

The realization among God's people that there could be more to life than the physical, temporal dimension gradually dawned.  Please read Ecclesiastes 9:4-6, which shows us that Solomon, with all his wisdom, did not understand that there would be more to life than his limited view showed him. God had not yet revealed to him the resurrection of the dead. He thought that only what he could experience in the flesh was the extent of life.  Various opinions developed over the years as to what the destiny of man would be at the time of his first death.  The example of Enoch in Genesis 5:24 was not understood.  *"Enoch walked with God; then he was no more, because God took him away."*  And even though they had the example of Elijah being taken up by chariots of fire, in 2 Kings 2, they had not yet understood where he had been taken.

At the time of Jesus' earthly ministry, the Jews were separated into two opinion camps concerning life beyond the present condition.  The Pharisees were of the opinion that there was a resurrection of the dead.  The Sadducees claimed that there was no resurrection; when you die, it is over for good. Jesus settled that question in word and in action. In Matthew 22, Mark 12, and Luke 14, stories are recorded where Jesus confirmed life after the first death. In the Matthew and Mark accounts, the Sadducees try to play mind games with Him over whose bride would be the woman who had married and lost seven successive brothers. Jesus spoke very clearly on both accounts. First, he said that people would be quite different, like angels, after the resurrection and would not marry. Second, He said clearly that there is a resurrection, quoting God saying,

> But about the resurrection of the dead—have you not read what God said to you, "I am the God of Abraham, the God of Isaac, and the God of Jacob"? He is not the God of the dead but of the living (Matthew 22:31-32).

The quotation from Luke does not address that contrived situation by the Sadducees. Instead, it is Jesus teaching at a Pharisee's house about showing off your charity and self-importance. Of course, Jesus knew that the Pharisees accepted resurrection in their philosophy, and so He assured them that they need not struggle for recognition and reward in this life. He said,

> But when you give a banquet, invite the poor, the crippled, the lame, the blind, and you will be blessed. Although they cannot repay you, you will be repaid at the resurrection of the righteous (Luke 14:13-14).

## Eternal Judgment

Now almost everyone who is a Christian these days believes in the resurrection of the righteous, but not very many understand the resurrection of the unrighteous. Read Matthew 25:31-46. In this passage Jesus gives a very clear description of the ultimate end of mankind.

> When the Son of Man comes in His glory, and all the angels with Him, He will sit on His throne in heavenly glory. All the nations will be gathered before Him, and He

will separate the people one from another as a shepherd separates the sheep from the goats. He will put the sheep on His right and the goats on His left . . . then they (goats) will go away to eternal punishment, but the righteous (sheep) to eternal life.

Please read that whole passage very carefully. Identify yourself with the sheep, but be sure to note that there are goats, plenty of goats. There are Christians who have been deceived into thinking that death for the unrighteous means oblivion, just evaporating away into nothing. This is not true, and for those who find this option more attractive than the struggle of being a Christian, it is a disaster. For the unrighteous, there is the Lake of Fire, prepared for the devil and his angels and all of the unrighteous whose names are not found written in the Lamb's Book of Life. The Lake of Fire means *EVERLASTING, NON-STOP PAIN*. Read from Revelation 20:7 through 21:8 for confirmation of this. It is one of the last things Jesus revealed to John in this book. Both the righteous and the unrighteous will exist forever. The righteous will exist in a glorious new life without pain or mourning with Jesus. The unrighteous will exist with the devil and his angels in the lake of burning sulfur and will be tormented day and night for ever and ever.

It is a very simple matter, as you have previously learned, to avoid the Lake of Fire and get into the Marriage Feast of the Lamb. Simple, but not easy. Those who teach that the Christian life is supposed to be easy and careless are not helping to prepare you for reality. Life is difficult and full of excitement and danger as a Christian, but it is possible to endure and be victorious through Jesus. As a heathen, life is impossible, and defeat is inevitable. Remember always that your reward is waiting for you at the end of the struggle. The following passage comes after a description of the trials and tribulations of God's people throughout the ages, from Abel through the prophets, and how they endured.

These were all commended for their faith, yet none of them received what had been promised. God had

104 • Foundations for the Christian Life

planned something better for us so that only together with us would they be made perfect. Therefore, since we are surrounded by such a great cloud of witnesses, let us throw off everything that hinders and the sin that so easily entangles, and let us run with perseverance the race marked out for us. Let us fix our eyes on Jesus, the author and perfecter of our faith, who for the joy set before Him endured the cross, scorning its shame, and sat down at the right hand of God. Consider him who endured such opposition from sinful men, so that you will not grow weary and lose heart (Hebrews 11:39-12:3).

# DIGGING DEEPER
## Resurrection of the Dead

1. Before Jesus came, did men understand that there was to be eternal life?

_____

_____

2. Can you cite a passage in Scripture that shows that Solomon did not understand eternal life?

_____

_____

3. Where did Enoch and Elijah go?

_____

_____

4. What did the Sadducees believe about resurrection?

_____

_____

5. Did Jesus say there was or was not a reward at the end of this life?

_____

## Eternal Judgment

6. Read 1 Corinthians 3:10-15 and then explain what it means to you.

_____

_____

_____

_____

7. Tell what you understand from Matthew 26:31-46.

_____

_____

_____

_____

8. Read John 3:16 and Revelation 20:7-21:8. Tell which category you fall into and how you know it.

_____

_____

_____

_____

9. How long will you exist?

_____

10. Describe where the devil will go at the end of the age.

_____

_____

_____

11. Who will reside with the devil when he enters his kingdom?

_____

_____

12. Describe where you will be when the devil gets his final reward.

_____

_____

13. In the passage from Hebrews 11:39-12:3, what is the key word?

_____

# IN HIM WE LIVE
# AND MOVE AND HAVE OUR BEING

## Founded Upon the Rock

You should know by this time that this series of lessons is about life and not about religion as it is practiced in the world today. I have not, do not now, nor will I ever urge you to *join a church*. That is a nonsense statement. The Church that Jesus founded, and is building, is not something you can join. It is a state of being. When you enter into the Christian life by means of the blood of Jesus, you become a part of the Church. The Church is the Body of Christ. It is a living organism which transcends organization and customs.

Let me repeat those thoughts in a slightly different way and add to it somewhat so that you will not be confused like many others are. The Church is not a human organization. It cannot be compared to a corporation or a service club. It does not share the attributes of a government or an army. Again, the Church is a living organism; it is the Body of Christ in which each of us who are part of it has a function and a place. It is like a family in which all members are sons and daughters. You did not join your family; you were born into it. You did not choose the place you are in the Body of Christ any more than your big toe decided to be what it is.

You have been born into the Body of Christ by your second birth. You were called and experienced godly sorrow for your sins and your ungodly life. You were granted repentance, you turned away from your past life, and came into submission to the King of the universe—Jesus Christ. He forgave you and granted you eternal life as you submitted to the waters of baptism. Jesus filled you with the Holy Spirit and gave you gifts with which to live a successful life of service. You have learned about the basic rudiments of Christianity, and now you are ready to begin using what God has given you in the way that He wants you to use it, for His Kingdom, for His glory. He, Jesus, is the rock upon which the Church is founded (see 1 Corinthians 3:11). He also is the One who puts you and me in the places He desires and gives us the functions that He requires of us. See 1 Corinthians 3:5-9, 12:4-13, and Ephesians 4:11-13. You and I are bought at a price—the blood of Jesus (1 Corinthians 6:19-20). If all of this is true for you, you are ready, God willing, to move on. If any of this is untrue or incomplete for you, stop now and go back. Get it all straight now.

It is important for you and me to have all of this straight before we try to go on. Frankly, it would be better for many to abandon Christianity from the start rather than try to live it under false pretenses. Trying to be a Christian on your own terms rather than God's is a frustrating and losing proposition.

## Gathering Together

It may astonish you to know that there are thousands of groups who gather together and call themselves some form of the Christian Church. Many of these groups will tell you that they are *the* church. What is more likely is that they are a small portion of *the* church. In biblical terms, the Church is *the people called out* by Jesus. There is never more than one church mentioned in Scripture for each city. Every Christian in a given city is part of the church of that city. This means that denominations have no standing with God at all; they are a means of division which is an offense to God. Non-denominational groups who proclaim some sort of elitism or separation from one another are also out of line.

The Scripture says,

> Let us not give up meeting together, as some are in the habit of doing, but let us encourage one another—and all the more as you see the Day approaching (Hebrews 10:25).

It is important for us to meet together for the purpose of encouragement and fulfilling those duties which God gives us. It seems clear that, since the Body of Christ is like a family (Ephesians 3:14), we should behave much as a family does. We should be personal and intimate, and that absolutely requires small groupings. For about 300 years after Jesus founded His Church, it met primarily in people's homes. One of the big reasons for the difficulties that we modern Christians experience is the size and impersonality of our gatherings. It is impossible for us to even know, much less be in a family relationship with, hundreds or thousands of others. Our master Jesus could do anything. In the matter of gathering, He chose twelve men, their dependents, and a number of unattached women to be His gathering. Although He was God, He was also subject to human limitations. The Scriptures say that He was a man in every sense except sin. At the end of His ministry and the beginning of His Church, there were about 120 people gathered together. Jesus did not set down strict guidelines for this, but it seems to be practical and prudent for us to keep these numbers in mind as we enter into the activity of being *church*. My personal recommendation is for every Christian to be attached to a *house church* gathering since that is where I have seen the Spirit of God working to form the loving family relationships that God desires.[1] There is help available for those who are called to enter into those kinds of relationships.[2]

In any case, as a Christian, you are called to gather with other Christians regularly so as to do—individually and together—what God directs. Since what we are doing is being formed into a family, then it is also important that we gather for purposes other than *religious* meetings. Christians certainly ought to be getting together for meals, recreation, and just to be together. There is strong evidence that gathering for these non-religious purposes is just as important to the Christian life as gathering for worship and teaching.

## The Wholeness of Life

Modern industrial society first separated men from the land. It has also piled men on top of each other in such numbers that they have become strangers to each other in massive quantities. In recent times the political and social movements have attacked the family and the structure of life. Life, for countless people, is chaotic and meaningless. It is made up of unconnected and isolated experiences between strangers. Even the most fortunate of us have lives made up of insulated blocks designated as recreation, career, spiritual, family, and so forth. This is unreal and unnatural.

*Separation of Church and State* is one of the silly statements which define our foolish age. If we understand what the church is then we can see that in order to separate church and state, we must get rid of all Christians in the exercise of government. Of course, that is the real objective of those who despise Jesus and, of course, it is impossible unless Christians allow it. If you and I can stop being Christians during our involvement in government or anything else, we are false Christians. Whether you are an artist, a garbage collector, or an astronaut, you are a Christian at every point in your life. The Scripture is full of admonitions like *"Rejoice Always"* and *"Giving Thanks Always"* and *"Praying Always."* Life is not divisible. God is involved in every bit of your life. It is up to you to be involved with God in every aspect of your life.

Resolve now to be in agreement with God on the wholeness of life. Pray and work toward unity in families and in the church. Pray that men will be united in righteousness before God.

## The Work

If you have not heard it before, you will hear of *"the Great Commission."* Just before He went back to the Father, Jesus said,

> Then Jesus came to them and said, "All authority in heaven and on earth has been given to me. Therefore go and make disciples of all nations, baptizing them in the name of the Father and of the Son and of the Holy Spirit, and teaching them to obey everything I have commanded you. And surely I am with you always, to the very end of the age" (Matthew 28:18-20).

This is the Great Commission: go and make disciples of everybody and teach them to obey what Jesus taught. Simple, right?

This means that we are to learn all of the things that Jesus taught us to do and then do them. It means that we are simultaneously to go out and get everyone else and gather them in as well, teaching them all that we have learned. It means that everyone is a disciple and everyone is discipling others. We are responsible to know and do and teach. There are no bystanders, observers, or spectators. Nobody gets off the hook by giving ten bucks instead of doing the work. You do the work and give the ten bucks as well. We all have a place and responsibilities. Jesus' program doesn't work unless we all work. It seems crazy because obviously Jesus could do the work Himself much better and much faster. In spite of that fact, He wants us to do it, and He gives us the authority and power to do it. We can do nothing without Him, and He will not do it without us. It doesn't matter that we don't understand very well, it is His decision. He said, *"God had planned something better for us so that only together with us would they be made perfect"* (Hebrews 11:40).

## Obedience

George Washington Carver was a great, southern, black educator. He established a very high quality university in Alabama just after the U.S. Civil War starting with few resources other than his faith in God. A story about him relates that once a northern reporter went to visit him for an interview. The reporter was required to wait outside Mr. Carver's office for a long time very early in the morning. Finally, he complained and asked what Mr. Carver was doing in there alone. The secretary said, "Mr. Carver goes in there every morning at 7:00 a.m. He prays until God gives him his directions. Then he comes out and spends the rest of the day doing what God told him."

It should be clear that neither the Scriptures nor Christian practices and traditions can specifically cover everything that will come up in our lives. We certainly do have sufficient guidelines to avoid sin and live in a godly fashion, but we do not have a pat answer to every problem and situation in our lives. For that, the Lord has provided His Spirit. He expects us to be obedient. In order to live a full and victorious life, we must live in the Spirit.

In 2 Corinthians 10:5 it says that,

> We demolish arguments and every pretension that sets itself up against the knowledge of God, and we take captive every thought to make it obedient to Christ.

Of course we will only communicate with the Lord Jesus by means of His Spirit since that is the way He set it up for us. In John 14:15-18, Jesus promised that He would send the Spirit. In John 15:26-27, Jesus said a little more about the Spirit. In John 16:5-16, Jesus told what the Spirit would teach.

We are able to know what God wants from us and for us on a daily basis by talking with the Holy Spirit. The kind of direction we can expect will certainly run counter to the world and its traditions. It will be godly direction toward unity and love in our families, our church, in everything. It is not an easy course to take, but it is the only course which will please God.

## Prayer

*Pray constantly* is the admonition you will find in 1 Thessalonians 5:17. It is guaranteed that the more you pray, the more you will grow in your Christian life. Countless stories can and should be told about the benefits of prayer. Prayer is a subject that is extremely large in scope. There is personal prayer and group prayer. There is prayer in the Spirit and prayer with the understanding. For the purposes of this book, it will suffice to say that prayer is one of the most important parts of the Christian life. Every Christian should set aside quality time each day to be in communication with God in prayer.

## Service

In Acts 2:42-47, there is a description of some of the ingredients of the lives of those who became believers at that time. We should remember that there was extreme persecution of Christians then, yet the body of believers grew rapidly in numbers and strength. What they did is worth noting and imitating.

> They devoted themselves to the apostles' teaching and to the fellowship, to the breaking of bread and to prayer. Everyone was filled with awe, and many wonders and miraculous signs were done by the apostles. All the believers were together and had everything in common. Selling their possessions and goods, they gave to anyone as he had need. Everyday they continued to meet together in the temple courts. They broke bread in their homes and ate together with glad and sincere hearts, praising God and enjoying the favor of all the people. And the Lord added to their number daily those who were being saved.

There are eleven important verbs in that short passage:

1. **Devoted** *to teaching, fellowship, breaking of bread, and to prayer.*

2. **Filled** *with awe.*

3. *Many wonders and miraculous signs* **were done.**

4. *All believers* **were** *together.*

5. **Had** *everything in common.*

6. **Selling** *possessions and goods.*

7. **Gave** *to everyone with need.*

8. **Meet** *everyday in the temple.*

9. **Broke** *bread in homes.*

10. **Ate** *together.*

11. **Praising** *God.*

Those are the things done by the first Christians with great success. The final statement reflects what the people around them did—*holding them in great favor*—and what God did, *adding to their numbers daily.* May God grant us the grace to imitate them successfully.

## DIGGING DEEPER
### Founded Upon the Rock

1. Jesus said, *"I am the way and the truth and the life. No one comes to the Father except through me"* (John 14:6). Please explain what that means to you in terms of how you intend to live from now on.

_____

_____

_____

_____

_____

2. Explain what you understand about Peter as the rock in Matthew 16:18 and Jesus as the rock in 1 Corinthians 3:9-10. How do these two passages relate to each other?

_____

_____

_____

_____

_____

3. You have entered the Body of Christ by what means? (See John 3:3)

_____

_____

## Gathering Together

4. Is it important for Christians to meet together?

_____

5. How many churches are there?

_____

6. Is it better to have a large group or a small one for a Christian meeting?

_____

## The Wholeness of Life

7. In what part of your life is it okay to ignore Jesus?

_____

## The Work

8. Who is responsible for making disciples of all nations?

   _____

9. If you are embarrassed or afraid to witness about Jesus, you can just give money so that others can do that part, right?

   _____

10. Do you know what kinds of things you are called to do in the body of Christ?

    _____

    _____

    _____

## Obedience

11. Can we know what God wants us to do on a daily basis?

    _____

    _____

12. What are two ways we can know what God requires of us?

    _____

    _____

## Prayer

13. How do you plan to be discipled in prayer?

    _____

    _____

    _____

## Service

14. After you have read Acts 2:42-47 and the exposition of it in the lesson, tell what bearing that will have on how you proceed with your life in Christ.

_____

_____

_____

_____

_____

15. Are you satisfied that you are prepared to go on with Jesus _no matter what?_

_____

_____

_____

16. How may we help you? (Take all of the space and time you need for this question and discuss it thoroughly with your teacher.)

_____

_____

_____

_____

_____

_____

Congratulations! You have completed this foundational course in Christianity. It is not the only foundational course. There are many others. Whatever you do, do not let elitism or exclusion into your life. Jesus is about inclusion and bringing all who will into unity, so that is what we should be about also. Completion of this course means that you have *begun* not *finished* the real course, which is life itself.

Continue to study the written and spoken Word of God; stay in close relationship with other Christians; worship God in Spirit and truth; serve the least of Jesus' brethren; and pray. God is able and faithful to complete the good work that he has begun in you.

If you desire to do so, you may contact the author at:

John G. Gill
Right-Of-Way
8726 Northbank Drive
Ventura, California 93004

---

[1] *How to Start a House Church* by Frank B. Smith, Crushed Grapes Publishing, P.O. Box 3009, Vista, CA 92085. This is the best of a number of works on house gatherings.

[2] *The Church in the House — A Return to Simplicity* by Robert Fitts, Preparing the Way Publishers, 2121 Barnes Ave. SE, Salem, OR 97306, 2001; and *Leadership-Servanthood in the Church* by Nate Krupp, Preparing the Way Publishers, 2121 Barnes Ave. SE, Salem, OR 97306.

# Preparing the Way Publishers

makes available practical materials
(books, booklets, and audio tapes)
that call the Church to the radical Christianity
described in the Bible.

Some titles include —
*The Way to God*
*Basic Bible Studies*
*Getting to Know GOD*
*New Testament Survey Course*
*Mastering the Word of God – and Letting it Master You*
*You Can be a Soul Winner – Here's How!*
*The Church Triumphant at the End of the Age*
*New Wine Skins – the Church in Transition*
*God's Simple Plan for His Church – a Manual for House Churches*
*Leadership–Servanthood in the Church as found in the New Testament*
*Woman – God's Plan not Man's Tradition*
*Restoring the Vision of the End-times Church*
*The Church in the House – A Return to Simplicity*
*God's Word Puts the Wind in My Sail*
*Foundations for the Christian Life*

For further information, see the PTW web page
at www.PTWPublish.com

For a free catalog and order form contact —

## Preparing the Way Publishers
## 2121 Barnes Avenue SE
## Salem, OR 97306-1096, USA

phone 503/585-4054
fax 503/375-8401
e-mail <kruppnj@open.org>

# Knowing GOD Series *from Preparing the Way Publishers*

The Knowing GOD Series consists of five study books. Each one takes you deeper in your knowledge of God's Word and in your relationship with Him. You do not need to do the series in the given order (1-5), but you may find that helpful.

**#1  Basic Bible Studies** • ISBN 1-929451-02-4 • 80 pages . . . . . . . . . . . . . . . . . . .**$9.95**
*A question-and-answer type, foundational Bible study book about the Christian faith.*
*Chapters include:*

1. Is There a God?
2. The Issue of Sin
3. What Provision Did God Make For Man's Sin?
4. How Should Man Respond to God's Provision?
5. Abiding in Christ
6. The Christian and God's Word
7. The Christian and Prayer
8. The Christian and the Holy Spirit
9. The Christian and Warfare
10. The Christian and Witnessing
11. The Christian and the Home
12. The Christian and the Church
13. The Christian and Business Affairs
14. The Christian and Discipleship
15. The Christian and Service
16. The Christian and the Return of Christ

**#2  New Testament Survey Course** • ISBN 1-929451-03-2 • 234 pages . . . . . . . . .**$15.95**
*This is a very unique 47-lesson Bible study survey of the New Testament.*

- It covers every verse of the New Testament
- It leads you in an in-depth study of each book. You will read the entire New Testament and either answer summarizing questions or summarize the book, a paragraph at a time.
- It harmonizes the Gospels so that you study Jesus' life in a single, chronological narrative.
- It places the letters in the order in which they were actually written.
- This study gives you background information on each book of the New Testament.
- You will apply each book to your own life situation.
- You will decide on verses to memorize from each book.
- You will know the New Testament when you have finished this study!

**#3  Mastering the Word of God - and Letting It Master You!**
ISBN 1-929451-04-0 • 46 pages . . . . . . . . . . . . . . . . . . . . . . . . . . . . . . . . . . . .**$5.95**
Workbook • ISBN 1-929451-09-1 • 34 pages . . . . . . . . . . . . . . . . . . . . . . . . . .**$4.95**
*This book is about various methods of in-depth Bible intake: how to hear, read, study, memorize, and meditate on the Word of God. With this book you will learn how to study the Bible. You will be able to develop a life-long plan of in-depth Bible study - mastering God's Word, and letting It master you.*

**#4  Getting to Know GOD** • ISBN 1-929451-05-9 • 288 pages . . . . . . . . . . . . . . .**$19.95**
*A devotional Bible study book on 57 aspects of GOD's Person, Character, and Attributes: His love, His mercy, His faithfulness, His goodness, His glory and majesty, etc. For each attribute, you will read an introduction, prayerfully read three or four pages of appropriate Scripture verses, answer study questions, do research, meditate on and apply the lesson to your life, memorize verses of your choice, and pray a closing prayer. This book was written by an actual Bible study group. This study will change your life!*

**#5  Qualities God is Looking for in Us** • ISBN 1-929451-06-7 • 384 pages . . . . . .**$23.95**
*A 53-week Bible study, devotional book on the qualities God is looking for in us: abiding in Christ, boldness, contentment, diligence, discipline, early riser, forgiving, generous, holy, honest, humble, obedient, praiser, prayer, servant, wise, zealous, etc. For each quality, you will read an introduction, prayerfully read three or four pages of appropriate Scripture verses, answer study questions, do research, meditate on and apply the lesson to your life, memorize verses of your choice, and pray a closing prayer. This book was written by an actual Bible Study group. This study will greatly challenge you!*

*Order Form on Back*

# ORDER FORM
### Preparing the Way Publishers
2121 Barnes Avenue SE, Salem, OR 97306, USA
Voice 503-585-4054 • Fax 503-375-8401
E-mail: kruppnj@open.org • Website: www.PTWpublish.com

## Knowing GOD Series

| QTY | TITLE | PRICE | TOTAL |
|-----|-------|-------|-------|
| _____ | #1 Basic Bible Studies . . . . . . . . . . . . . . . . . . . . . . . . . . . . . | $9.95 | _____ |
| _____ | #2 New Testament Survey Course . . . . . . . . . . . . . . . . . . . . | $15.95 | _____ |
| _____ | #3 Mastering the Word of God . . . . . . . . . . . . . . . . . . . . . . . | $5.95 | _____ |
| _____ | Mastering the Word of God Workbook . . . . . . . . . . . . . . . | $4.95 | _____ |
| _____ | #4 Getting to Know GOD . . . . . . . . . . . . . . . . . . . . . . . . . . | $19.95 | _____ |
| _____ | #5 Qualities GOD is Looking for in Us . . . . . . . . . . . . . . . . . | $23.95 | _____ |

## Other Books

| QTY | TITLE | PRICE | TOTAL |
|-----|-------|-------|-------|
| _____ | The Way to God . . . . . . . . . . .25¢ ea., 10 for $2.00, 100 for | $15.00 | _____ |
| _____ | You Can Be a Soul Winner—Here's How . . . . . . . . . . . . . . | $5.95 | _____ |
| _____ | New Wine Skins—The Church in Transition . . . . . . . . . . . . . | $2.00 | _____ |
| _____ | God's Simple Plan for His Church . . . . . . . . . . . . . . . . . . . . | $9.95 | _____ |
| _____ | Woman—God's Plan, Not Man's Tradition . . . . . . . . . . . . . . | $10.95 | _____ |
| _____ | The Church Triumphant . . . . . . . . . . . . . . . . . . . . . . . . . . | $12.00 | _____ |
| _____ | Leadership—Servanthood in the Church . . . . . . . . . . . . . . . | $4.00 | _____ |
| _____ | Mobilizing Prayer for World Evangelization . . . . . . . . . . . . . | $2.00 | _____ |
| _____ | Fulfilling the Great Commission by A.D. 2000 and Beyond . . . | $1.00 | _____ |
| _____ | Restoring the Vision of the End-times Church . . . . . . . . . . . | $14.95 | _____ |
| _____ | The Church in the House . . . . . . . . . . . . . . . . . . . . . . . . . | $9.95 | _____ |
| _____ | God's Word Puts the Wind in My Sail . . . . . . . . . . . . . . . . . | $13.95 | _____ |
| _____ | Foundations for the Christian Life . . . . . . . . . . . . . . . . . . . | $11.95 | _____ |

**Ordering Information:** Fill in your order and send it **with your payment** to Preparing the Way Publishers for processing. A new copy of this Order Form will be included with your order for your future ordering use.

**Payments:** To avoid extra bookkeeping and handling expenses, credits for less than $1.00 will not be sent. Prices are subject to change without notice. **Full payment is expected with order.**

## Postage and Handling for mainland United States orders:

| Amount of Order | P & H | Postage and Handling for Alaska, Hawaii, |
|-----------------|-------|------------------------------------------|
| Under $20.00 | $3.00 | U.S. possessions, and all other nations: |
| $20.00 - $39.99 | 15% | Actual postage charge plus 10% handling |
| $40.00 and above | 10% | |

**TOTAL Book Order** $_____

**Plus Postage & Handling** $_____

**GRAND TOTAL** $_____

## Ship To:

Name: _____ Date of Order: _____

Address: _____ Telephone:_____

City _____ State _____ Zip _____ Nation_____

Printed in the United States
4792